Prenatal Promises:
A Nine Month Devotional for Expectant Mothers

Jennifer Pruszinski

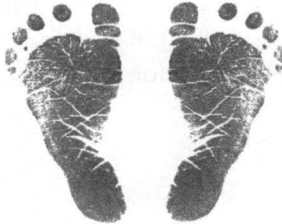

Lulu.

I0223539

PRENATAL PROMISES: A NINE MONTH DEVOTIONAL
FOR EXPECTANT MOTHERS

Copyright © 2008 by JLB, Wildwood Crest, NJ 08260

All rights reserved. No part of this book may be reproduced in any manner except for brief quotations in critical articles or reviews, without permission.

Scriptures quoted from *The Full Life Study Bible, New International Version*®, copyright © 1992 by Life Publishers International. Used by permission.

ISBN 978-0-615-24975-9

Forward

As an expectant mother I searched diligently for a pregnancy devotional. I really wanted and needed to set aside at least a few moments each day to talk to God about my baby. I wanted to focus my scripture reading, praying and quiet times on my pregnancy. I found a few books that were helpful in this endeavor but most of them were only designed to last 30 days - and I was going to be pregnant for over 280 days!

It was in between my pregnancies that I started *Prenatal Promises.* This book is designed to give expectant mothers a brief devotion for each day of pregnancy. Its nine chapters are focused around thematic promises that God gives us relating to pregnancy. Each chapter has 30 scriptures, reflections and prayers based on those themes. I pray that this book will enable you to grow closer to God as the baby He has blessed you with grows inside you.

Prenatal Promises:
A Nine Month Devotional for Expectant Mothers

Acknowledgements

With special thanks:

To my son Noah and my daughter Abbey for filling my life with joy, inspiring me to pray so much and giving me a reason to write this book.

To my husband Dereck for being a great partner, husband and friend for the past 15 years, and for being such a wonderful dad.

To my family for encouraging me in this project and all of my projects in the past 31 years. Your belief in me has kept me believing in myself.

To my editing team: Natalie, Linda, Maria and Kathy. I greatly appreciate all of your help and suggestions.

To my sisters in Christ at Celebration Community Church for the prayers you've invested in this project, in my children and in my life.

To my colleagues in D1-a for your support, opinions, layout and font help.

To my pastor Carlos Martinez for growing me in Christ and for introducing me to the wonder that is Lulu Publishing Company.

To my sister Linda and my niece Brooke for making *Solomon Says* a reality and letting me know this really could be done.

To my brother Steven for making *carpe diem* a part of my life and making Heaven a place I can't wait to get to. Sorry it's not a coffee table book.

Month 1:
The Promise of a Gift

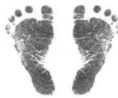

Day 1

Genesis 1:28 *God blessed them and said to them, "Be fruitful and increase in number; fill the earth and subdue it."*

Although there is no doubt in my mind that God's will for my life is for me to be a mother, His word first confirms this for me in His command to Adam and Eve. Even though they failed to resist temptation, God's love for His creation prevailed. So much so that He commanded Adam and Eve to multiply so that His love could grow. In the same way, as a parent you may face pain in some way. You may be disappointed by your children and their disobedience at some time. But your love for your children must supersede your hurt. God promises to forgive us for our sins when we disobey Him and we must do the same for our own children. We increase our numbers so that our love may grow and this should be our primary focus in parenting.

Lord, I know that I may face pain, disappointment, anger or hurt on account of my child but I know that I can count on You to sustain me and be my peace in difficult times. The child You've given me is a great expression of Your love. Please help me to be the parent You have called me to be. I pray that the love I have for my child will always supersede any negative emotions that may arise in our lives. I ask You today for the strength to forgive my child just as You have forgiven me. In Jesus' name I pray. Amen.

Day 2

Genesis 4:1 *Adam lay with his wife Eve and she became pregnant and gave birth to Cain. She said, "with the help of the Lord I have brought forth a man."*

Cain was the first human born on earth, the son of Adam, who was created by God's breath and dust, (Genesis 2:7) and Eve, who was created from Adam's rib (Genesis 2:22). Eve was the first woman to experience conception and delivery and at this point had also been cast out of paradise. Nonetheless, she attributed the birth of her son to God. It was through God's help that Cain, the first man born on earth, came to exist and it was also through God that your child has come into existence. It is only through His help and with His help that we are able to bring forth life.

Lord I praise You as the author of Life. I recognize the need for Your power in the fragile process of conception and birth. I ask You to give me the same help that You gave to Eve so long ago. Please guide me through the process of birth. I do not want there to be one minute when my baby and I are out of your care. Help me to maintain a healthy pregnancy and a safe delivery and help me to care for this child that You have blessed me with in a way that brings glory to You. In Jesus' name I pray. Amen.

Day 3

Genesis 17:6 *"I will make you very fruitful; I will make nations of you and kings will come from you."*

It is the Lord who makes us "fruitful." He gives us the ability to conceive, carry and deliver. In this verse, God promises Abraham and indirectly his wife Sarah, that their lives would be fruitful and that they would become the parents of the nation of Israel. Although I like being a part of a large family, I do not know anyone who would like to "make nations," nor are many of us monarchs that would give birth to royalty. However, I do know that each of our children is more important to us than an entire nation and each child becomes king or queen of our motherly hearts. God not only gives us the physical ability to be mothers, but also the emotions that are unique to this relationship.

Lord, it is You who is the Creator of nations and King of the universe. I praise and thank You for the opportunity to be a part of Your nation and Your kingdom. I also thank You for giving me this baby and for the unique relationship between mother and child. I pray for our relationship now and ask that You would bless its future. Please let my baby always feel my love and know how much I care about him or her. In Jesus' name I pray. Amen.

Day 4

Genesis 17:16 *"I will bless her [Sarah] and will surely give you a son by her. I will bless her so that she will be the mother of many nations; kings of peoples will come from her."*

Sarah waited so long. Talk about patience! She was ninety years old when she bore her son Isaac. I know people who are trying to get pregnant and to them the months of trying can seem like an eternity. Imagine what all those years felt like to Sarah! Not only did she have to wait so long but at such an old age she must have had concerns about her health and the health of the baby. Women today who conceive after age 35 are cautious with their pregnancies, had the technology been available, I'm sure Sarah would have been a candidate for amniocentesis. So why did God wait so long to give her a son? Did she do something in her life to keep her from being rewarded sooner? God's timing and motives are beyond my knowledge, but this situation makes me wonder if we would even remember much about Sarah if she had given birth to Isaac at, say age 25. However, I do know this- Sarah is still remembered today and most of all for the very fact that she waited so long for a baby. Isaac's birth proved to Israel and to the world that God is faithful. He keeps his promises and He can do anything.

Lord, please give me some of the patience that Sarah had. I know she struggled and tried to manipulate her situation, taking matters into her own hands by giving her servant to her husband so he could have a child by her, but 90 years is such a long time! Lord, help me use this pregnancy to develop the fruit of patience in my life, whether I'm waiting to conceive or deliver, or even for a good night's sleep. Please let me rest in Your timing. In Jesus' name I pray. Amen.

Day 5

Genesis 18:14 *"Is there anything too hard for the Lord? I will return to you at the appointed time and Sarah will have a son."*

This is the question of all questions and a rhetorical one at that. Of course nothing is too hard for God. But I think that the most important part of this verse is not the initial question, but the phrase, "appointed time." God had an appointed time for Isaac and he has one for you and your baby as well. He promised to give Sarah a son and He did. Likewise, He promises perfect timing for your pregnancy and the blessings He has and will give to you.

Lord, I know that You have an "appointed time" for the events in my life and I don't pray that those times are changed, but that my will and my idea of an appointed time will coincide with Yours. I will answer the question that You posed to Abraham so many years ago. No! Nothing is too hard for You and I pray now that I can live my life with this answer in the forefront of my mind. I pray for Your perfect timing to reign over the life of my baby as well. Please give him (her) to me at the perfect time and let his (her) life be blessed with the gift of Your schedule. In Jesus' name I pray. Amen.

Day 6

Genesis 21:1 *Now the Lord was gracious to Sarah as he had said and the Lord did for Sarah as he had promised. Sarah became pregnant and bore a son for Abraham.*

God keeps his promises. This is as much a tried statement as it is true. God blessed Sarah with his grace and she became pregnant. And while God does not promise that each of us will deliver a child, He does promise us the gift of his grace. As Paul writes, *And He said to me, My grace is sufficient for you* (2 Corinthians 12:90). God's grace is all that we need and I encourage you to seek it daily.

Lord, You've told me through Your Word that Your grace is sufficient. I pray now that You would bestow that grace on me and my baby. You grant us with numerous promises that are stated in Your Word and fulfilled in Your Son. Please fulfill these promises in my life and let the first be the gift of grace. I also ask for an extension of this grace for my baby. Please let Your Spirit fall upon him (her) and bless this child as he (she) grows inside me and comes into this world as Your living gift to me. In Jesus' name I pray. Amen.

Day 7

Genesis 21:6 *Sarah said, "God has brought me laughter and everyone who hears about this will laugh for joy."*

God blessed Sarah with the gift of her son Isaac and along with him came the gift of laughter. I wonder how long Sarah had gone without laughter in her life, consumed with the absence of a child. With his birth came joy- an emotion that had probably become strange to her as well. Had she been perfect, she would have been filled with the Lord's joy in all situations, just as we are to be filled with the joy of Christ (John 15:11). But oh how it must have felt to hold her son in her arms! I'm sure she experienced tears of joy along with her laughter.

Lord, I thank You for the joy that You have given me in my life. You gave me the gift of salvation through Your son, Jesus Christ and this gift brings me the purest joy. It is renewable daily and everlasting. I also thank You for the added joy that my child has already brought and will continue to bring into my life. I ask you today that You would give him (her) the gift of joy as well. Please give him (her) an optimistic outlook on life and fill his (her) days with many moments of joy and laughter. In Jesus' name I pray. Amen.

Day 8

Genesis 30:20 *"God has presented me with a precious gift."*

When Leah saw her son Zebulun for the first time, she proclaimed that God had given her a precious gift. Here is another example that God gives us in His Word of a godly woman and mother. Whether we are experiencing our own trials and stresses of life or expectancy, God's Word provides a perfect model for each of our lives. Whatever trials our present circumstances might bring, there are Biblical examples, such as Leah to whom we can turn for guidance. Leah teaches us that our children are a gift, a precious gift presented to us only from the Lord. How special we must be to be chosen for this honor!

Lord, I know You have given me many gifts throughout my lifetime, both material and immaterial and I praise You for these, knowing that the most precious gift You have given me is Your Son. I thank You for the salvation You've given me through His living sacrifice. I also thank You for the honor I have from being chosen to receive the gift of my own child, who is as precious to You as he (she) is to me. Please renew in me daily the joy I will feel when I look into his (her) eyes for the very first time, knowing that he (she) will be given to me as a blessed gift from You. In Jesus' name I pray. Amen.

Day 9

Genesis 33:5 *"They are the children God has graciously given your servant."*

In the Old Testament, there are many references to children and descendents being blessings from God. The connection between God and the blessing of children was very clear. In this verse, as Jacob meets his brother Esau, he describes the people with him as children given to him by God. Jacob clearly knew that all blessings in life came from God, especially the gift of children. And although children may hold a different value in today's society, the connection between God and the blessing that He gives us in the form of children is no weaker. God is still the means by which we are blessed and the children given to us continue to be blessings in our lives.

Lord, I thank You for the many blessings You have given me in my life. I know that all of them come to me directly from You. I thank You today for the child You have blessed me with. Like Jacob, I know that he (she) has been graciously given to me from You. However, I have found that in my life knowledge does not always result in action. Lord, I desire to parent this child in a way that recognizes him (her) as a blessing in my life and as a gift from You. In Jesus' name I pray. Amen.

Day 10

Deuteronomy 1:11 *May the Lord, the God of your fathers increase you a thousand times and bless you as he has promised.*

Could God increase me a thousand times? If He wanted to He could and I'm sure if I traced back my ancestry, I could find a thousand people who have descended from one couple. However, this has never been my own prayer. I'm the type of person who stands in awe of the mother of twins, and even someone like my grandmother, the mother of six. My prayer is this: that God would bless my child in a way that would enable him (her) to be part of a strong line of descendants, that he (she) would have deep family connections and live long enough to continue his or her family line. But, most of all I pray that my son (daughter) would live a blessed life that honors God.

Lord, I do not ask You to increase me a thousand times, but I do ask that You would preserve my family so that our heritage would run deep and that my child would be connected to a strong and fruitful family tree. Maybe one day my descendents will number a thousand, but to me, their number is not as important as their strength. I ask today for Your blessing on both my child and my descendents and my ancestors. May we be a family tree that is nurtured by Your Word and by knowledge of You. In Jesus' name I pray. Amen.

Day 11

Deuteronomy 7:13 *He will love you and bless you and increase your numbers. He will bless the fruit of your womb.*

The Lord loves His children. This love will manifest itself in many ways: our relationships, our careers, our talents, etc. The blessings He gives us, however, may come slowly or in disguise. In Deuteronomy 7:13, He has promised to bless us and to increase our numbers. Our children will be and are a blessing in our lives as we increase in numbers and pounds. We are living proof of this promise.

Lord, You have promised Your love to us, even when we don't deserve it. Please enable me to express the same unconditional love to my child. You show us Your love in countless ways and through numerous blessings. One of the most powerful ways You have blessed me is through the gift of this child. You have given this baby to me and I thank You for this promise and its fulfillment in my life. In Jesus' name I pray. Amen.

Day 12

Deuteronomy 28:11 *The Lord will grant you abundant prosperity- in the fruit of your womb.*

Prosperity is not usually a word associated with babies. In today's world, we often think of children as depleting our bank accounts. But in God's eyes our prosperity is not based on our bank accounts. He counts us wealthy based on our hearts and minds. If they are focused on Christ, they are invaluable. Likewise, one of our strongest assets can be found not when we count our dollars, but rather, when we count the sleeping heads in their beds at night or the number of plates set around the dinner table.

Lord, I seek to be prosperous in Your eyes. Please give me a heart that desires what You define as valuable. Let me be faithful and obedient. Let me be filled with the Spirit of Jesus Christ. And please let me see how valuable my child is. I not only want to be aware of his (her) value, but I also want him (her) to know for sure that he (she) is valuable to both me and You. Help me to show him (her) daily that he (she) is priceless in my eyes, worthy of my attention and my affection. In Jesus' name I pray. Amen.

Day 13

1 Samuel 1:11 *"O Lord almighty if you will only look upon your servant's misery and remember me and not forget your servant but give her a son, then I will give him to the Lord for all the days of his life."*

In the first book of Samuel, we meet another woman distraught with infertility. Hannah prayed for a son and waited patiently for God to answer her prayer. And as if waiting to be blessed with a child wasn't hard enough, Hannah also had to withstand the taunts of her husband's other wife. In the society that I live in, I could not imagine sharing my husband with another wife, which would seem to be an extremely stressful situation in itself. Not only did Hannah have this burden, but she was additionally tormented by Peninnah's provocations. I would imagine that a situation such as this could easily produce in Hannah all degrees of anger, rage, depression and the like. But of the many ways Hannah could have acted out against her adversaries, she did nothing. For me, Hannah expresses the epitome of God's patience. Being patient means doing nothing. As one of the fruits of the Holy Spirit, it is a supernatural power that God gives us so that in tough situations we can have the power to do nothing. Resting in Him and waiting on Him is God's will for us and Hannah's life is a perfect example of how this patience is not only possible, but also ultimately rewarding.

Lord, I thank You for the example of Hannah that Your Word provides for me. Her life perfectly models the fruit of patience that You call me to enjoy in my life. She was able to rest in Your presence and Your power. Lord, I pray for the same patience in my life. I know that patience is a specific fruit given to me through Your Holy Spirit. I cannot experience this gift without Your provision. Lord, please provide me with this fruit and help me to rest in Your perfect will and timing, both throughout this pregnancy, and also as I journey into motherhood. In Jesus' name I pray. Amen.

Day 14

1 Samuel 1:26 *"As surely as you live my Lord, I am the woman who stood here beside you praying to the Lord. I prayed for this child and the Lord granted me what I asked of him. So now I give him to the Lord for his whole life he will be given over to the Lord."*

At times I have found myself bargaining with God. "Oh Lord, if You would just do this, I promise to…" Although I always have good intentions, I can't always say that I have been able to keep up my end of the bargain or that this was an appropriate tactic to use with God. In the first book of Samuel, we find Hannah making a similar promise to God. Hannah asks God for a son and in turn promises to give her son over to God. Hannah was faithful in her bargain with the Lord. When I read how she gave her son up just after he was weaned, I thought she had made the ultimate sacrifice and wondered if I could ever voluntarily go through something so heartbreaking, even if it was my end of a bargain with God. A deeper study of Hannah's situation has revealed to me that she wasn't in complete despair when she brought her son to the house of the Lord in Shiloh. She did get to see Samuel grow in strength and wisdom, but just not under her own care. Hannah knew that it was God's will for both their lives and was therefore able to rest in His answered prayer and her own obedience. I was able to become pregnant without making such a bargain with God, but I do acknowledge that my child belongs to God. Yes, I get to care for him (her), but ultimately he (she) is a child of God and I must raise him (her) with this in mind, and with the hope that he (she) too will give his (her) life to God in whatever way he (she) is called.

Lord, You have given me a number of responsibilities in life, none greater than caring for my child. I praise and thank You for this responsibility and I ask for the wisdom and strength to raise this child to be one of Your own. I want him (her) to use his (her) life for Your purposes. Please give my baby the ability to hear Your calling for his (her) life and the courage to obey You as he (she) hears it. I ask that You would guide us as we grow together. In Jesus' name I pray. Amen.

Day 15

Psalm 113:9 *God settles the barren woman in her home as a happy mother of children. Praise the Lord.*

Yes, praise the Lord, for He has provided us with the many joys of motherhood. This psalm describes a mother as "settled." We have seen many women, from Sarah in the first book of the Bible to Elizabeth in the New Testament, who have struggled with infertility. Although their lives as barren women might have been what we would describe as successful, they were still unsettled. They longed to be "happy mothers of children," and God gave them a great peace through answered prayer. It was only God's peace that was able to settle the yearning of their hearts.

Lord, I praise You for my role as a mother and for fulfilling the longing of my heart. The joy I experience as a mother is like no other. There will be trials, I know, but these struggles will enable me to grow both closer to You and closer to the mother You want me to be. Thank You for settling me as a happy mother of children and giving peace to my heart. In Jesus' name I pray. Amen.

Day 16

Psalm 127:3 *Sons are a heritage from the Lord. Children are a reward from Him.*

At some time during your pregnancy, you will undoubtedly hear the phrase "children are a blessing from the Lord." However, the most important time that this phase is spoken is through the voice of God, who refers to children as His heritage and His reward to us. When we think of rewards we think of an exchange- one is usually rewarded in exchange for some sort of action on his or her part. The person who finds a lost puppy is given a reward. The caller that tips off the capture of a criminal is likewise rewarded. Does this exchange hold true for pregnancy as well? It can be, as this verse states, but it can also be so much more. It may be that our children will give us rewarding lives, or that what seems to be a stressful time at one moment will turn out to be rewarding in God's time. The truth is that God rewards on a divine level. His point system, like His timing, will not always coincide with ours. What will always coincide however is His divine plan and timing for our lives and the lives of the unborn. This psalm does not intend to answer our questions of the who, when and why of pregnancy, but it is a message from God, who here enumerates one of the many ways He will bless us in our lives.

Lord, I thank You today for the rewards of life, especially this child. Please help me to recognize that You reward us on a divine level, in Your perfect timing and in accordance with Your will. Please enable me to be a good steward of the blessings You have given me. In Jesus' name I pray. Amen.

Day 17

Psalm 127:4-5a *Like arrows in the hands of a warrior are sons born in one's youth. Blessed is the man whose quiver is full of them.*

If I were a warrior, and let's just say for the record that I'm not, I would definitely want a quiver full of arrows. When one's profession is fighting and killing, there is no better possession than an arrow. In fact, the more arrows a warrior has, the better off he will be. For in this situation, arrows are the difference between life and death. And so, here God speaks to us through His Word, telling us that when He blesses us with children He is giving us a gift of life, a gift that is a blessing as valuable as our own lives.

Lord, again I thank You for the blessing of my child. Your Word speaks of his (her) value, comparing children to the powerful arrows of a warrior. I do not consider myself a warrior, but as a mother, I have days when I can feel the toil of battle. Lord, I ask You for strength in those days. Please help me to remember that it is You who has blessed me with the powerful gift of this child. I pray that he (she) will be the arrow that keeps my role as a mother focused and I praise You for the blessing You have given me in this life. In Jesus' name I pray. Amen.

Day 18

Psalm 128:3-4 *Your wife will be like a fruitful vine within your house, your sons will be like olive shoots around your table. Thus is a man blessed who fears the Lord.*

When I sit down to eat a meal I hardly ever think about the origins of the food. How does broccoli grow? How was this cheese made? These types of questions rarely enter my mind, probably because I'm so removed from the food production process. Even homemade cooking has taken on a new definition, in my kitchen anyway; it usually means adding water, eggs and 350 degrees of heat for forty minutes. But when I look at the metaphor this psalm delineates, I see that at one time food played a vital role in the success of a household in general. Therefore, the connection that people had with their food was much stronger. A house with fruitful vines in its yard and full cupboards in its kitchen was defined as a successful one. A man with such a household was a blessed man. This psalm describes a house filled with many children as just as satisfying as one filled with food and wine.

Lord I thank You for my home and for the convenience in my life, especially when it comes to food preparation. You are the great Provider and just as You provide me with actual fruit and food in my life, I know that this child in my life is just as satisfying a gift from You. Thank You for blessing me with the gift of this child. In Jesus' name I pray. Amen.

Day 19

Psalm 144:12 *Our sons in their youth will be like well nurtured plants and our daughters will be like pillars carved to adorn a palace.*

In this verse we are again reminded of the value that God places on our children. He likens sons to well nurtured plants and daughters as pillars. These may seem like strange analogies, but not any stranger than ornaments, bridles or arrows, as we've seen before. A well nurtured plant is valuable for the fruit it will produce. It is strong and productive and the prized possession of its owner. Just how is it that a plant becomes well nurtured? It is nothing short of the hard work of the gardener who prunes, waters and feeds the plant in order to ensure its successful growth. Similarly, daughters are likened to pillars, not just any pillars, but ones specifically carved to adorn a palace. A palace is one of the most important buildings in a society, used to house its most important people. Pillars are not just what are used to hold up such buildings, but are also the first things seen as the building is approached. Put this way, we can see that God has crafted our sons to be strong and productive and has carved our daughters to be just as strong, upholding their households.

Lord, You have crafted my child with his (her) own purpose, including being a blessing in my life. I thank You that You have crafted him (her) perfectly to fit this role. I ask that I would remember him (her) always as a treasured possession, crafted by You. Just as a gardener spends so many hours striving for a well nurtured plant and a sculptor spends so much time carving pillars, please enable me to give my child the same kind of attention, so I can raise him (her) to fulfill the very purpose You've ordained for him or (her). In Jesus' name I pray. Amen.

Day 20

Proverbs 17:6 *Children's children are a crown to the aged and parents are the pride of their children.*

Upon first glance, this proverb seems straight forward-children are crowns, parents are proud. But when I look at it closely, I see that it says much about the triangular relationship among grandparents, parents and children. The first part talks of children's children being a crown to the aged. In my life, I have seen this in the way my grandparents have treated me and also in the way my parents dote over my children. Their eyes light up when they enter the room. It is the same light that greets me even today when I go to visit my grandparents and it's wonderful. The second part of the proverb says that parents are the pride of their children, not that parents are proud of their children, which is true, but is not what is being expressed here. It is very seldom that I, as a parent, think of myself as the pride of my son, but if this is true, I must conduct myself in a manner that will make my child proud. This means, most of all, acting as a godly parent, on direct assignment from God to care for His child.

Lord, I thank You for the relationship that I have with my grandparents. I love being a crown in their lives. And I also thank You for the relationship that my child has and will continue to have with his or her grandparents. I know that he (she) will love being a crown in their lives as well. I ask that You would strengthen and maintain the relationships that form this triangle, that we as children, parents and grandparents would consider ourselves a blessing in each other's lives. I also ask You to help me be the kind of parent that makes her child proud. Of course I know that at some point, probably around age eleven, it is inevitable that my child may be embarrassed by me. However, I desire to parent him (her) in such a way that he (she) will not be ashamed or disappointed to have me as his (her) mother and I know that I can only do this with Your help. Lord, please keep our relationship strong and most of all, please help me to be the kind of parent to this child that glorifies You. In Jesus' name I pray. Amen.

Day 21

Isaiah 8:18 *"Here I am and the children the Lord has given me. We are signs and symbols in Israel, from the Lord Almighty who dwells on Mount Zion."*

If there is any question about where children come from, besides the technical birds and the bees explanation, it is answered for us in the book of Isaiah. God uses this prophet to describe the relationship between God and His chosen people, Israel, through the metaphor of a mother and her baby, which will be explored more in later months. Here the prophet identifies children as being given by the Lord. Our children are God's children and we receive them as a gift from Him.

Lord, I thank You again for the blessing of this baby. I know he (she) has come straight from You. Although I have thanked You for him (her) many times before, the joy he (she) will bring me is never-ending and will be renewed daily and thus should be my thanks and praise to You. How grateful I am to be the recipient of such a precious gift. Lord, I pray that as I kneel before You carrying my child, we would be signs and symbols of Your love in our lives. In Jesus' name I pray. Amen.

Day 22

Isaiah 44:3 *"I will pour out my spirit on your offspring and my blessing on your descendents," says the Lord."*

In this verse God promises to pour out His Spirit on our children and to bless our descendants. Is there anything more we could ask for in life? Genius or superstar talent? God does not promise that your child will carry out your dreams- either those that you have left unfulfilled or those you have stitched together for him (her). What God does promise however, is that your child will have His Spirit poured out onto him (her) and that he (she) will be blessed. This is the type of prayer we should pray for our sons and daughters. Of course we can include specifics, but when all is said and done, isn't a child blessed by God all or more than we could ever dream?

Lord, You have promised to pour out Your Spirit on my offspring and to bless my descendants. I lay claim to that promise today. Please bless my baby and sanctify him (her) with Your Spirit. What more could I ask for? In Jesus' name I pray. Amen.

Day 23

Isaiah 49:18 *"Lift up your eyes and look around, all of your sons gather and come to you. Assuredly as I live," declares the Lord, "you will wear them as ornaments; you will put them on like a bridle."*

I know that not all children may seem to come at the perfect time or in the perfect situation in our lives as we see it. However, I also know that all children come to life in God's perfect timing and in God's perfect situation. He tells us that we will wear our children as ornaments, and He's not just talking about mothers' charm bracelets and birthstone rings. Our children are what we decorate our lives with, who we pride ourselves in and who represent us in the best and worst ways.

Lord, I know that ornaments and bridles were very prized possessions in Biblical times. They therefore represented the same treasured spots in our hearts that You set apart for our children. And although we might define treasure through different means today, nonetheless, there is no greater treasure than the gift of a child. Lord I accept this gift from You and I ask You to help me treasure my son (daughter) in both easy and difficult times, knowing that any gift from You is more valuable than any earthly prize. In Jesus' name I pray. Amen.

Day 24

Luke 1:24 *After this his wife became pregnant and for five months remained in seclusion. "The Lord has done this for me," she said. "In these days he has shown his favor and taken away my disgrace among the people."*

Struggling with infertility today can be discouraging, even devastating. In the first chapter of Luke, we meet Elizabeth, the future mother of John the Baptist, Jesus' cousin. She, like so many other women of the Bible, not only wrestled with the absence of a child, but was also forced to deal with the disgrace that such an absence caused within their societies. Elizabeth is the last woman documented in the Bible with the struggle of infertility and again it becomes evident that God took this disgrace from her and blessed her with the gift of a son. From Sarah to Elizabeth, God has been faithful with His blessing of children.

Lord, You are the great provider. You have answered an infinite number of prayers, specifically enabling me to conceive this child. By answering prayers, You make Your love for me even more evident. You cared about both Elizabeth's public disgrace as well as her desire to be a mother and You care about me and my child just as much. You do not desire for me to suffer from public disgrace, infertility or any pain. Yet my life is not painless. Although You are not the cause of pain in my life, You do permit it at times. And I pray to You for those times, that I may seek You for peace and know that You are ultimately in control. In Jesus' name I pray. Amen.

Day 25

Luke 1:31-32 *You will be with child and give birth to a son, and you are to give him the name Jesus. He will be great and will be called the son of the Most High. The Lord will give him the throne of his father David, and he will reign over the house of Jacob forever. His kingdom will never end.*

The Lord gave Mary the gift of His son. When she first heard this news she questioned it because of her virginity. The Angel Gabriel assured her that the Holy Spirit was to come upon her because "nothing is impossible with God" (Luke 1:37). This gift came to Mary at a time we would consider to be awkward at the least. She was a virgin and engaged to a man named Joseph, who had to also be convinced by an angel that this child was from God and that he was not to divorce her for adultery. The timing in this situation, however, like all situations, was God's. Because Mary conceived before she was married, she was able to fulfill the prophesy given in Isaiah, *The virgin will be with child and will give birth to a son* (Matthew 1:23). The circumstances had to be perfect for God to act in Mary's life. They may or may not have seemed perfect to her, we only know her response, *I am the Lord's servant* (Luke 1:38).

Lord, I thank You for the perfect example You have given me in Mary. She was a true servant of Your will. Because of Your timing, she conceived at a time in her life where she could have been overcome with shame. However, Mary was strong and thus was blessed with a son, not just any son, but the Son of God. She knew that even though the circumstances did not seem perfect to the world, she was bestowed with a great honor, not just the honor of giving birth to the Son of God, but the honor of serving and obeying God in her life. This is the same attitude that I want for myself and my child. Please give us the hearts of servants. Let us obey and serve You as parent and child, resting in Your wisdom and timing for our lives. In Jesus' name I pray. Amen.

Day 26

Luke 1:41 *When Elizabeth heard Mary's greeting, the baby leaped in her womb and Elizabeth was filled with the Holy Spirit. In a loud voice she exclaimed, "Blessed are you and blessed is the child you will bear."*

Every baby born into this world is a blessing to his (her) family, but none more than the baby in Mary's womb. Jesus' birth was a gift in the life of his mother, and more so to the rest of humanity. For all of creation, Jesus' birth, life and death have provided the hope of eternal life through His living sacrifice for the debt of our sins. And because of this we are able to experience great joy in our lives. However, the initial joy that Jesus provided was to his family- and here specifically to his mother, aunt and unborn cousin.

Lord, I praise You for the blessed child I have in my womb and for the many blessings his (her) life will provide for me and my family. I also thank You for the blessing of Your son, born in human form to Mary in Bethlehem and killed on a cross for my sake in Jerusalem. Both His life and His death have been a blessing in my life and have given me joy in the promise of an eternal future. Thank You for this gift. In Jesus' name I pray. Amen.

Day 27

Luke 2:22 *When the time of purification, according to the Law of Moses had been completed, Joseph and Mary took him to Jerusalem to present him to the Lord.*

Just as Hannah gave her son to God in the first book of Samuel, 600 years later Mary and Joseph present their son to the Lord. Presenting the Son of God to God might seem to be a redundant act. However a closer study of this event might reveal that when Mary and Joseph presented their son to the Lord, they were setting a model for future parents of the world. Mary and Joseph were conscientious followers of the Jewish faith. They followed Jewish custom and tradition in their lives. Therefore, waiting for the appropriate time and following the specific guidelines of the Jewish Law, they presented their child to the Lord. In the same way I encourage you to formally present your child to God. Is it necessary for a child's salvation? Of course not, but when I look at this event in Jesus' life, I know that I wouldn't want anything less for my own child. Formally setting your child apart for God makes it clear to your family and friends that you acknowledge the role of God as co-parent in your child's life, that you realize that he (she) is a blessing given to you from God and that you will do all you can to raise him (her) in a way that glorifies his (her) creator.

Lord I praise You again for my child and I ask that when the appropriate time comes, I would present him (her) to You in a way that would please You. I want it to be publicly known that this child has come from You and belongs to You. Please enable me to continue that dedication past the day of the ceremony and into his (her) life so that I may raise my child in a manner that is also pleasing to You and acknowledges that he (she) is a child of God. In Jesus' name I pray. Amen.

Day 28

Luke 18:5 *Jesus called the little children to him and said, "Let the little children come to me and do not hinder them, for the kingdom of God belongs to such as these. I tell you the truth, anyone who will not receive the kingdom of God like a little child will never enter it.*

Although Jesus never physically conceived a child of His own, children played an important part in His ministry. In this chapter of Luke, Jesus showed His disciples that children are a blessing because they represent the attitude we should have in our lives. We are instructed to receive the kingdom of God as a child does- with unquestioning faith and innocence. These children were not a bother to Jesus, as His disciples first thought, but rather, became a perfect model for Him to illustrate His desire for our own hearts and minds.

Lord, I pray that I will continue to receive the kingdom of God in my life as a little child- with open arms, an open heart and an open mind. I also pray that my child would accept Your kingdom and Your gift of salvation early in his or her life. I ask that he (she) would establish a strong relationship with You as he (she) begins his (her) walk with You and that through the work of the Holy Spirit, he (she) will bring more people to accept You as well. In Jesus' name I pray. Amen.

Day 29

Hebrews 6:14 *"I will surely bless you and give you many descendants," says the Lord.*

God promises to bless us with many descendents and this promise has come true in your life with you and your child. There are many ways that the Lord blesses His children. One way is through the ability to have children of our own. God promises not only to bless us in this way but extends this blessing to include our entire ancestry. When I think back to my own ancestors, I wonder how they would react to my life and I know that when I see the span of my family through the generations I am amazed at the many blessings God has given us. These blessings become most clear when we are able to look back on the incidents that seemed so dreadful at the time of their occurrence but worked out for the best in God's plan and in God's time. I ask you today to face your future and your blessings with the same assured vision that you use to look back.

Lord, this child is a blessing and I thank You for him (her). Please continue to bless us as we continue together for the next few months. I also ask for Your blessing on this child throughout his (her) life and the lives of our descendents. Let us be a family that pleases You both now and in the many years to come. In Jesus' name I pray. Amen.

Day 30

Hebrews 2:13 *Here am I and the children God has given me.*

This verse is a prophesy first given by Isaiah in the Old Testament and fulfilled by Jesus in the New Testament. Initially we see that children are a gift given from the Lord. When we see this verse repeated in a letter to the Hebrews, Jesus is quoted as saying, *Here am I, and the children God has given me.* This same sentence takes on a different meaning the second time around. Here, the author of the letter is describing the relationship that Jesus has with the human race. Jesus was transformed into human form so that through His sharing in humanity, His death would free believers by granting them eternal life. Jesus died as a living sacrifice for the sins of all humanity, so that by confessing our sins and believing in Him we may escape death through eternal life. Because Christ experienced our humanity, we can count ourselves not only as His brothers and sisters, but also as His children.

Lord, I thank You for the gift You have given me in Jesus Christ. Because He became human in every way, His death was able to make atonement for the sins of His children. I thank You for the gift of eternal life that I have been given through His death and resurrection and I pray that my child will accept Jesus as his (her) savior as well. I praise You for being able to count myself one of Your children and ask that my child will also lay claim to the right to be called a child of God. In Jesus' name I pray. Amen.

Month 2:
The Promise of Life

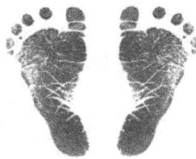

Day 1

Genesis 1:27a *So God created man in His own image. In the image of God He created him; male and female He created them.*

God created each of us in His own image. And our creation begins with the process of ovulation. When the level of estrogen is sufficiently high in your body, usually around day thirteen of the menstrual cycle, a matured egg drops into the fallopian tube where fertilization can take place. The egg can survive in the fallopian tube for about twelve to twenty-four hours. If it is not fertilized, it will be released as part of menstruation. If, however, it is fertilized, it becomes an embryo and implants itself in the lining of the uterus, where the baby God gives you begins to develop.

Lord, I thank You today for the miracle of the human body. You have designed humans to be able to reproduce as part of Your will and I praise You for that. Lord I ask for Your blessing today on the process of ovulation which is the first part of conception. Please bless the egg that has been released in my body. I pray that it will be healthy and strong and that it will have the perfect environment in which to become an embryo. I pray that in Your perfect timing and under Your provision the process of development will continue. In Jesus' name I pray. Amen.

Day 2

Genesis 2:7 *The Lord God formed the man from the dust of the ground and breathed into its nostrils the breath of life and man became a living being.*

When God created the first man, He took some dust from the ground and breathed life into it. From God's breath, Adam came to life as a human being. Eve was then formed from Adam's rib. Cain, the third human was formed in the same way that every human has been formed since, through the process of conception. Once ovulation has taken place, sperm needs to be transported into the fallopian tubes. The sperm needs to be able to accomplish some difficult tasks including surviving the hormonal environment of the vagina and penetrating the cell membrane of the egg. Once this happens, the egg becomes fertilized and is then known as an embryo.

Lord, the process of conception is dependent upon so many variable factors, including timing and environment. Successful conception is based on the coming together of so many events that we should be in awe every time a baby is actually conceived. I pray that Your sovereignty would reign over this process in my baby. I ask that Your perfect plan and timing would prevail in the creation of this new life. Please set up the perfect time and environment for the formation of this embryo. Lord, I trust in Your perfect will and timing for this baby's life. In Jesus' name I pray. Amen.

Day 3

Genesis 5:1 *When God created man, He made him in the likeness of God.*

We have been created by God and to resemble Him. The process that God has chosen to form beings that best reflect Him begins with conception and then undergoes the stage called implantation. Once a mature egg is penetrated by a strong sperm, it becomes an embryo. After the embryo is about five days old, it "hatches" out of its shell and begins a process of cell division called the blastocyst stage. During this process the cells that will develop into a fetus separate from those that will form the placenta, as the embryo moves out of the fallopian tube and into the uterine cavity.

Lord, You have created each of us in Your likeness and I praise You for being honored to live as a creature that reflects Your holy being. Lord, I know that You have overseen the process of implantation that has taken place as my baby has been created. Please help the cells of the embryo to divide properly so that the fetus and the placenta will grow healthily. I ask that the embryo has safely found its way from my fallopian tube to my uterus. In Jesus' name I pray. Amen.

Day 4

Deuteronomy 10:14 *To the Lord your God belong the heavens, even the highest heavens, the earth and everything in it.*

As we see in the beginning of Genesis, God created heaven, earth and all that they possess, including each human being, for God is the author of life. Each life begins with the process of conception and implantation. About 13 days after conception the embryo is approximately .2 millimeters in size and the formation of blood and blood vessels in the embryo begins. The embryo also becomes connected to the placenta by what will soon be the umbilical cord. The next process to take place is called gastrulation. In this process, the embryo begins to form three layers. Each layer will be responsible for forming all of the systems and parts of the body. The endoderm layer will form the lungs and the digestive tract. The mesoderm layer will form the muscles, bones, heart, lungs, reproductive and excretory systems. The ectoderm layer will form the skin, nail, hair, eyes and all parts of the nervous system.

Lord, I praise You for You are the Author of Life. You have created all of the inhabitants of heaven and earth, just as You have created the baby within me. I ask that as my baby undergoes the process of gastrulation, You would oversee the development of his or her body. Lord, as this little embryo forms blood and blood vessels, I pray that he or she would have healthy blood, with no infections or diseases. Additionally, as the embryo begins to form layers, I pray that each layer would be a strong support for all of the systems and parts of the body. Please enable the endoderm, mesoderm and ectoderm to properly form and grow. In Jesus' name I pray. Amen.

Day 5

Deuteronomy 32:18 *You deserted the Rock, who fathered you; you forgot the God who gave you birth.*

Even though human males father and human females physically give birth to babies, it is God who puts the process of life in motion and enables it to stay in motion. God is ultimately responsible for each life on earth both physically and spiritually. When each life has been in existence for about nineteen days, the embryo is between one and one and a half millimeters in size and begins to take on a pear shape with the head being wider than the tail end. A neural plate begins to form, creating a neural groove that will be the precursor for the nervous system, and is one of the first organs to develop.

Lord, I praise You, for You are our Father and it is You who has brought each of us to the point of birth. Likewise, You oversaw the fathering of my child and will be with us as I bring him (her) to the point of birth. Lord, as my baby prepares to form his (her) nervous system, I pray that You would bless this formation. The nervous system contains the brain, the spinal cord and neurons. It is the system of the body that controls the body's communication system. His (her) nervous system will control all of his (her) thoughts and movements. Lord, as this system is beginning to be formed, I pray that he (she) will have a strong nervous system and that there will be no problems in the way that his (her) brain works or the way that it communicates with the rest of his (her) body. In Jesus' name I pray. Amen.

Day 6

Job 12:10 *In His hand is the life of every creature and the breath of all mankind.*

God is not only in control of the beginning of our lives but maintains control as our lives continue on earth. He provides us with our life initially and renews this provision daily. He breathed into dust to create Adam and continues to sustain us through His breath of life as we live out His will for us on earth. As God's hand reaches out to your embryo the baby will begin to form a primitive streak which is an indentation that runs a third of the length on the embryo. A head fold will rise on either side of this base. Additionally, blood vessels will begin to form for the newly emerging blood cells and muscle cells will begin formations and fusion for early heart development.

Lord, I know that the life of my child is in Your sovereign hand and I praise You for the power it holds. You will prepare my baby with the body he (she) needs to take his (her) first breath and will help him (her) to take that breath. I also ask that as You begin to form his (her) head and heart, his (her) development will be blessed. I ask that his (her) head and brain will be formed without any complications and that his (her) heart will be strong. Please give my baby a healthy heart without any murmurs or weaknesses. In Jesus' name I pray. Amen.

Day 7

Job 33:4 *The Spirit of God has made me; the breath of the Almighty gives me life.*

It is God who has created us and it is His breath that sustains us. Even though we may not feel Him breathing on us, His presence and Spirit give us life and enable us to maintain it for as long as He has purposed. As God's creation grows to three millimeters, it begins to develop cells that will become eyes and ears. Additionally, an endocardial S-shaped tube begins to form. This tube makes the heart asymmetric and cardiac muscle contractions begin.

Lord, You have made my child and You will give him (her) breath. As the cells of his (her) embryo continue to develop I pray that they would be excellent foundations for his (her) eyes and ears. I ask that he (she) would have no vision or hearing problems. Please form these parts with the ability to perform the purpose for which You have designed them. As my baby's heart continues to form, I ask that You would strengthen it. The heart is the organ of life and I pray that my baby's will be strong so that it will be able to sustain his (her) life both in the womb and out of it. In Jesus' name I pray. Amen.

Day 8

Psalm 24:1 *The earth is the Lord's and everything in it, the world and all who live in it.*

Whether or not humans accept their position as children of God, the entire earth and all who inhabit it belong to God. We are His creations and He has created our bodies in such a way that we are able to reproduce. Just the idea of creating and carrying another human being inside us is miraculous. Most people proclaim the miracle of birth as they deliver their baby into the world, but I also believe that the onset of life alone is a miracle. Typically the human body will reject foreign bodies as a means of protecting itself, but God, in all His cleverness created a "loophole" in the system that enables the body to accept an embryo that attaches itself to the uterus. As the embryo moves into the lining of the uterus, it pushes aside some cells, destroys others and taps into maternal blood vessels, using your blood for its own nourishment. And although the embryo's tissue is very different than your own, your immune system has been divinely designed to accept and nurture this new being.

Lord, I thank You for the way You have designed our bodies. I know that we were created in Your image. Lord, I praise You for giving me a body that is able to reproduce and I am grateful for the ability to create, carry and deliver this baby. Lord, I pray to You now asking that as this baby continues to find a place to grow inside my body, he (she) would be easily nurtured and supported by my body. Please create the perfect environment inside me so that my baby can have the strongest and healthiest of beginnings. In Jesus' name I pray. Amen.

Day 9

Psalm 36:9 *For with You is the fountain of life; in Your light we see the light.*

      In the Bible, God draws many parallels between life and light. He is the Giver of life and of light. Life that is truly blessed is filled with the light that He provides. When we reflect His light in our lives, our lives become fulfilled in a unique and perfect way. God's light is the fountain that provides us with life. When your baby is first given life, the "fountain" that is the source of his (her) life is called the placenta. This vascular structure provides the embryo with oxygen and nutrients that nourish the baby until it is born. Your placenta, which is formed during the first four weeks of life, enables your baby to grow and develop until he (she) is able to be nourished by you.

      Lord, I praise You for Your role as the Fountain of Life. You are the light of the world and as I allow Your light to shine in me, I will reflect Your light to the rest of the world. Please help me to do this in a way that honors You. Lord, as my baby grows inside me, a placenta is developing which will be a fountain of life for my baby, allowing him (her) to receive oxygen and nutrients as he (she) grows within me. I pray that the placenta will be perfectly formed and would be a viable source of nutrients for my child. Please keep my placenta in perfect working order, and keep it in its proper position so that I will not suffer from placenta previa. In Jesus' name I pray. Amen.

Day 10

Psalm 65:18a *But be glad and rejoice forever in what I will create.*

God is the Creator of life and as He gives us the gift of life, we are to rejoice and be glad, for as our children are born they begin to fulfill God's will for their lives. As your baby develops from egg to embryo to fetus to a "full grown" baby you have little control over this process. It is important to stay healthy by eating nutritious foods, exercising and getting proper rest. But even if you do everything "by the books" your little one will still follow the development that God has planned for him (her). Because we live in a fallen world, we as humans are susceptible to developmental difficulties, injuries and sicknesses. Although these may seem unbearable to us as parents, with God's help, our hearts can be changed so that we can enable our children to live out God's will for his (her) life no matter how difficult it may seem.

Lord, You are the Creator of my child and I know that You have created this baby in your image and that You have a specific plan for his (her) life. I ask that as he (she) is created, he (she) will be free from all health or developmental problems. If it is Your will for him (her) to have mental or physical challenges I pray that I would be able to accept Your will and trust in Your sovereignty. Lord, I may ask myself, "Why would God let this happen?" And I pray now that I would be answered with Your peace and love. Please enable me to be glad and rejoice forever in what You have created. In Jesus' name I pray. Amen.

Day 11

Psalm 104:30 *When You send Your Spirit they are created, and You renew the face of the earth.*

God sends His Spirit to create His children and as God's spirit reaches out to your baby, he (she) becomes encapsulated in a type of water-tight balloon sac, called the amnion. Fluids from your body fill the sac, creating amniotic fluid which makes the perfect cushion for the embryo. This sac and its fluid will protect your baby from all of the bumps, jerks and overall movement that you engage in through your busy days. Additionally, the amniotic fluid keeps a consistent temperature for the baby and provides a weightless environment that lets the baby move around and even exercise within you.

Lord, I ask that as You send Your Spirit upon the creation of my child, You would remain with him (her) as he (she) is enclosed in the amnion. I pray that this baby would be protected by this enclosure as he (she) grows. You have designed my body to create the perfect cushion for this child and I ask that it would protect my baby as he (she) grows inside me. You know that I have a busy and stressful life Lord, and that I'm constantly on the go. I ask that I would take no action that would hurt my child. Please keep me from the temptation of working too hard, becoming over-stressed or denying myself sleep. I also ask that I would not decide to lift anything too heavy or put my body in any situation that would compromise the health of my child. In Jesus' name I pray. Amen.

Day 12

Psalm 119:73 *Your hands made me and formed me; give me understanding to learn Your commands.*

God reaches out His hands to create and form our children. As His hand is guiding the development of your baby, He is creating the sealing sign of your pregnancy, a tiny heartbeat. By the end of four weeks, your baby's initial heart begins to contract building up to a rate of 180 times a minute. Your baby's heart rate will slow down as the pregnancy progresses and will level out at about 140 beats per minute. As the heart forms, small capillaries and its blood vessels impede the blood. The baby then can receive more oxygen and therefore can rest his (her) heart from beating so fast. Listening to your baby's heartbeat for the first time either by ultrasound or fetoscope will not only be the first real sign of the baby living inside you, but may also invoke many emotions, one of which may be a feeling of a true connection with your baby's Creator.

Lord, I thank You for Your hand which has reached out to create my baby. I ask that that same hand would give my child an understanding of Your commands. I also pray again for the formation of my baby's heart. Please bless the arteries and tubes that form his (her) heart and give strength to his (her) heartbeat so that it will sustain his (her) new life. I ask that not only would You give him (her) a strong heartbeat, but also that You would give him (her) a heart that desires to understand and follow Your commands. In Jesus' name I pray. Amen.

Day 13

Ecclesiastes 11:5 *As you do not know the path of the wind, or how the body is formed in the mother's womb, so you cannot understand the work of God, the Maker of all things.*

The formation of an embryo in a mother's womb held much more mystery for the people of Biblical times than it does today. Modern science has taken much of the mystery out of the prenatal process. Even though I have researched the process myself, I am still awed by what takes place in a baby's birth. From the perfect timing and environment of the sperm and egg through the nine months of growth, I'm sometimes astounded by the fact that children are born at all. However, it doesn't take much to remind myself that there is a higher power controlling each element of life and that being is the Lord Almighty. It is He who oversees the process and truly gives power to our human bodies. Science can explain every detail on a technical level, but anyone who carries a child has to know that there is more to it than cells and hormones. There is a spiritual presence that laces the process together and brings each egg to life and that presence is that of God, our Almighty Father.

Lord, I pray for every pregnant woman in the world, that through the prenatal process, she would feel Your presence and know that You are God. Yes, there is a technical side to pregnancy and I pray for each stage of development in my baby, but I also know that it is Your Holy Spirit that provides life. There is an element of mystery in the process that makes it truly Yours. Lord, I ask that as You create this child in my womb, the process would bring me closer to You so that I would come to know You better and love You more. In Jesus' name I pray. Amen.

Day 14

Isaiah 42:5 *This is what the Lord God says, He who created the heavens and stretched them out, who spread out the earth and all that comes out of it, who gives breath to its people and life to those who walk on it, "I the Lord have called you in righteousness. I will take hold of your hand."*

It is the Lord that gives us breath and life as we walk on the earth He has created. There are numerous environments on earth, ranging from tropical to arctic as are there many kinds of shelters for humans ranging from caves and huts to mansions. During our time on earth, we may live in different environments and be protected by numerous types of shelters. However, God instructs us that our homes on earth are temporary and that we will truly be home when we join Him in heaven. No matter how varied our temporary homes here on earth are, they all begin in the same environment and in the same shelter, the interior upper portion of our mother's uterus. It is in this section of the uterus that the blastocyst implants itself for the first forty weeks of its life.

Lord, I praise You for Your provision. You have created the earth and all of the environments and shelters that it offers for those who walk on it. I also praise You because of the wonderful shelters that You have provided for me. I am blessed to feel so comfortable in my bed each night and I attribute that comfort to You. Thank You for all You have given me. Lord, I pray to You now asking that You would offer such comfort to my child as he (she) walks on the earth You have created. And I ask that no matter how comfortable we are we would always consider the temporality of our life on earth and seek our greater residence with You. In Jesus' name I pray. Amen.

Day 15

Isaiah 43:1 *But now this is what the Lord says- He who created you, O Jacob, He who formed you O Israel, "Fear not for I have redeemed you; I have summoned you by name and you are mine."*

When God creates and forms his children, He gives each one a unique design. This design, known as DNA, is transported through the head of the sperm and contributes to the unique genetic makeup of the child. Even though the size of the sperm is miniscule, measuring only .06 of a millimeter long, it contains all of what the male will contribute to the hereditary blueprint of the new baby. The rope-ladder pattern of DNA and protein contains either an X chromosome or a Y chromosome, determining whether the child will be female or male, respectively. Other characteristics contained in the DNA of the sperm include height, skin, eye and hair color, etc. The Lord has provided this complex, yet complete system so that each of His children are designed, not only in His image, but also with a unique genetic buildup.

Lord, I praise You for the supreme control that You have over science. And I ask that as the DNA of the sperm is entering into the egg to form my baby, the genetic blueprint that it forms will be exactly as You have planned it to be. You have not only summoned my child by name, but have also designed him (her) uniquely to be Your child. I ask that as the genetic process is taking place, there would be no window for deformity. Lord, please ensure that the perfect number of chromosomes are formed and that as the sex of my baby is being determined, there would be no ambiguity as to what the sex of the baby is. Please protect him (her) from all sexual defects. In Jesus' name I pray. Amen.

Day 16

Isaiah 49:5 *And now the Lord says- He who formed me in the womb to be His servant to bring Jacob back to Him and gather Israel to Himself, for I am honored in the eyes of the Lord and my God has been my strength.*

As your baby is formed in the womb, God is present. Sometimes you may find that the formation of your child takes what would seem to be a wrong turn. This event may result in a miscarriage. Miscarriages can take place for a number of reasons including damaged, too few or too many chromosomes. This is explained as nature's way of protecting itself against genetic deviations. I'm not sure why God would start a life and then end it. However, I know that *in all things God works for the good of those who love Him* (Romans 8:28).

Lord, I ask that You would give my baby a distinct purpose in life so that he (she) would live a long and fruitful life. Please protect this embryo from any damaged chromosomes. I pray that he (she) would have the perfect amount, not too few or too many and I ask that as he (she) develops, he (she) would find an environment that supports him (her) and enables him (her) to grow. Please take control of the growth process so that there would be no defects. Help my baby to grow and thrive within me. Please protect us from a miscarriage. However, if my child's life on earth is ended early I ask that You would give me the strength I will need to endure the situation. Please help me to trust in You and Your sovereignty. In Jesus' name I pray. Amen.

Day 17

Isaiah 57:16 *I will not accuse forever, nor will I always be angry for then the spirit of man would grow faint before me, the breath of man that I have created.*

It is God who creates your baby within you, giving him (her) the ability to take his (her) first breath, upon delivery into the world. But long before your baby takes his (her) first breath, he (she) may let you know that he (she) has arrived through many hormonal changes that you may experience. The first sign is usually a missed period, which is soon after accompanied by swelling, tender breasts, nausea and extreme fatigue. These symptoms are the result of the hormonal production of hCG or *human chorionic gonadotropin* and progesterone. And although they produce irritating symptoms, they also start and maintain all of the events of pregnancy that need to take place within the body for your baby to grow strong enough to take his or her first breath at birth.

Lord, I thank You for the life within me and for the hormones that my body is able to produce to sustain it. I ask that as my body becomes victim to these hormones, their effects would not be too severe. I know that every pregnancy experience is different and I ask that as these hormones take control of my body, the nausea, irritability and exhaustion that they may produce would not be overwhelming. Lord, please give me the strength to withstand this unpleasantness and to offer my suffering to You. Please encourage me as I grow this child within me. In Jesus' name I pray. Amen.

Day 18

Isaiah 66:2 *"Has not my hand made all these things and so they came into being?" declares the Lord.*

As God's creation comes into being, it is composed of cells. These cells, as small as they are, each have a specific job to do for the creation of the embryo. This foreknowledge is one that science cannot explain. God has created each cell with the same code built into the cell nucleus. However, different parts of this code are expressed in different cells. It is amazing how our bodies naturally grow and respond during the development of pregnancy. No matter how scientific doctors and researchers have made this process, it is truly a result of God's hand bringing each life into being.

Lord, I thank You for Your hand that has created everything in the world, including both me and my child. I ask You today to bless the cells that will grow into my child. Please let each cell know exactly what it is to become and help it to develop into the part it is designed to form. Lord, the power of creating a child belongs solely to You. However, in my era and culture it has become very scientific. Therefore, I ask You to give wisdom to my doctors. As I consult with them during this pregnancy, I pray that they will give me wise counsel and that they will guide me in my baby's growth. If there are to be complications during this pregnancy please instruct them on how to act in the best interest of both me and my child. In Jesus' name I pray. Amen.

Day 19

Jeremiah 18:16 *"O house of Israel, can I not do with you as this potter does?" declares the Lord. "Like clay in the hand of the potter so are you in the palm of my hand."*

The analogy of the clay and the potter is a very powerful one used by God to illustrate the dimension of our relationship with Him and made familiar to most of us through hymns and worship songs that incorporate the same analogy in their lyrics. This is such a beautiful way to think of the relationship that God has with your unborn baby as well. God is stretching out His hand in the role of the potter to form your child in your womb. The shape and purpose of the clay is solely in the hands of the potter and so it is with your child. God is forming him (her) in His own form and with His own purpose and because of this we rejoice.

Lord, I praise You for Your role as the potter and I ask that You would mold my child as Your valuable work of art. Please design him (her) in Your perfect form and for Your perfect purpose. Lord, I surrender my child to You today and ask that You would mold him (her) to be a child of God. Please help me to accept and to nurture the child that You have created so that his (her) life will bring glory to Your name. In Jesus' name I pray. Amen.

Day 20

Nehemiah 9:6 *You alone are the Lord.   You give life to everything and the multitudes of heaven worship You.*

The Lord gives life to everything, from the smallest creature to the largest. Each species is created with a unique composition. Man has been created by the Lord as a vertebrate. As embryos develop, forty small blocks of bone called somites are formed on each side of the neural groove. Thirty-two of these blocks become vertebrae while the other eight that make up the tail gradually recess.   Ribs will start to grow around the rudimentary lungs from the twelve vertebrae at the level of the baby's chest. All the vertebrae are held together by connective tissue and muscles which establish flexibility in the backbone. Nerves will also emerge from between the vertebrae and form a network throughout the body.

Lord, thank You for creating man to be a vertebrate. I praise You for all that my spine allows me to achieve each day and I ask that as this pregnancy and labor puts pressure on my back, You would protect it. Please keep me from suffering from any back pain. I also ask that You would protect my baby as his (her) vertebrae are being formed. Please give him (her) a strong back that is free from all paralysis or deformity. I also ask that You would guard over the nerves that will emerge from between the vertebrae and will reach out to every inch of his (her) body. I pray that they would each be formed in perfect working order. In Jesus' name I pray. Amen.

Day 21

John 1:4 *In Him was life and that life was the light of men.*

It is through Jesus Christ that we are given eternal life. His sacrifice on the cross provided the perfect blood sacrifice to atone for the sins of the world. Through acceptance of Him as our savior and confession of our sins, we are granted eternal life. It is this eternal life that provides light to men in a world of darkness. In terms of pregnancy, the darkness of your womb can now be lit for you through the procedure of an ultrasound. This slightly uncomfortable but painless process enables you to see your baby through the use of a machine called a transducer. Sounds and the echoes that they produce are transformed into moving pictures. So this enlightening process doesn't really use light at all. However, as early as six weeks into the pregnancy, it will enable you to see one of the most beautiful sights in the world, the tiny heartbeat of your baby.

Lord, I thank You first and foremost for Your Son. Through Him I have been given life and my gift of eternal life acts as a light in this world of darkness. I also thank You for the technology available to me today. Being able to invade the darkness of my womb to give light to my unborn child is an amazing process.   I ask that when I have an ultrasound examination, I would see a perfectly healthy baby. If there are to be any complications in this pregnancy, I ask that You would make them visible to the technicians and the doctors so that the proper steps can be taken to ensure development. In Jesus' name I pray. Amen.

Day 22

John 6:33 *For the bread of God is He who comes down from heaven and gives life to the world.*

On earth, we eat bread to maintain our lives. Without food we will die. Even with food, at some point in our life we will die. But our death does not have to mean the end of our being, for through the Son of God, we have been offered eternal life. Jesus is the bread of God. It is His body that has been given to us as a means for our life after death. As your baby grows in your womb it is nourished by the food that you eat. Pregnancy can bring on the desire to eat a lot of food as well as strange combinations of food. And although you do not want to gain an excessive amount of weight, it is important to maintain a high consumption of vitamin-rich rather than high-calorie foods. Fruits and vegetables, a variety of whole grains and high-protein foods make the healthiest diet for a pregnant woman and her unborn baby.

Lord, I praise You for providing me with the bread of God, which enables me to have eternal life. As I provide my baby with food while he (she) lives within me, I pray that I would be able to make smart food choices. I do not want to use this responsibility as an excuse to consume food like a vacuum cleaner, nor do I want to deny nutrients to my baby. Please help me to remember that everything I eat will enter into the embryo and to find a healthy balance of nutritious and delicious food in my diet. In Jesus' name I pray. Amen.

Day 23

John 6:57 *Just as the living Father sent me and I live because of the Father, so the one who feeds on me will live because of me.*

As your baby grows inside you, he (she) is fed through the umbilical cord and placenta which have been formed to provide nutrients and oxygen to the fetus. Everything you ingest will be transformed into an edible form for your child. And through the simple process of eating, you will be feeding your child. This type of feeding is automatic and therefore easy. However, after you give birth, the feeding process becomes more demanding as you choose between breast or bottle methods and then make the necessary preparations and give the time it takes to feed your baby, especially in the middle of the night. Eventually your child will graduate to jar food and then table food and your role as "feeder" will slowly decrease. But this role is only to feed the physical body of your child. He (she) also needs to be fed spiritually and this act involves consuming the food provided to us through the sacrifice of Jesus Christ. He promises us that when we feed on Him, we will receive eternal life.

Lord, I pray today for my child's nutrition. I ask that my body will provide him (her) with the perfect amount of nutrients so that he (she) will grow strong. I also pray for the feeding process that will take place once my baby is born. Please help me choose the right feeding method for us and enable me to develop a workable routine. Lord, as my child continues to eat by himself (herself) I ask that everything he (she) puts into his (her) body would be done so with the intention of glorifying You. I also pray that my baby will turn to You as the source of his (her) spiritual food so that he (she) will have an eternal life with You. In Jesus' name I pray. Amen.

Day 24

Acts 3:15 *You killed the Author of Life but God raised Him from the dead.*

God is the Author of Life. He has created the human species and has given life to each individual. As the life of our baby continues on, a face begins to appear. Tiny eyes, nose and mouth are being formed and the head, which had been inclined forward straightens itself up. The head still has no skull, so the brain is visible. The head of the embryo is also very large compared to the rest of the body. This is because the embryo grows from the head down. This largeness will continue throughout infancy. When the baby is born, his (her) head takes up about one quarter of the body, but in an adult the head is only one eighth of the body.

Lord, You are the Author of Life. I praise You for giving life to the baby within me and I ask that You would please bless the formation of my baby's head. As his (her) face is being formed, I pray that he (she) would have no deformities in his (her) small eyes, ears and mouth. As this baby's brain is being formed I also pray that it is free from all malformations and that the skull would be its perfect protection. Lord, give my child a healthy brain and a mind that seeks You throughout his (her) life. In Jesus' name I pray. Amen.

Day 25

Acts 17:24a *The God who made the world and everything in it is the Lord of heaven and earth.*

God has created the world and has filled it with many kinds of species. But He only created one creature with which to have fellowship, the human. He gives life to humans and as their creator, He has designed them to function and survive in the world which He has created for them. In order to protect our organs He has provided us with an outer covering called skin. This skin is formed at about 6 weeks of life. The skin covers the muscles, forming in two layers, the first is a thin layer called dermis and the second is called the epidermis which grows from the back forward. Both sweat glands and sebaceous glands develop in the epidermis. The skin becomes soft as tiny hairs grow from hair follicles within the skin.

Lord, I thank You for creating my child and the world into which he (she) will live his (her) life. I praise You for designing us with everything we need to survive. As my baby's skin is formed, I ask that You would bless its development. Please give my child healthy skin that will protect his (her) muscles and organs. I ask that his (her) skin would be free from any diseases and that he (she) would desire to take perfect care of it throughout his (her) life. In Jesus' name I pray. Amen.

Day 26

Acts 17:25 *And He is not served by human hands, as if He needed anything, because He Himself gives all men life, breath and everything else.*

The Lord has provided life for each of us and all we need to survive in the world. Just as He provides for the birds of the air and the flowers of the field, He supplies us with everything we require. God does not need anything from us in return. He does not *need* us to serve Him, but when we choose to serve Him we bring Him pleasure. Your baby's physical ability to serve the Lord begins in the womb. As your baby grows, very short arms and legs form, each with hands and feet that start to take shape.

Lord, I praise You for providing us with everything we need in life. And I ask that as my child grows You would see that his (her) arms, legs, toes and fingers would perfectly be formed and that he (she) would have all ten fingers and toes. I also ask that my baby would use his (her) hands to serve You. I know that You do not need to be served with human hands but I hope that he (she) would choose to use his (her) hands, feet, fingers and toes to serve You and to bring glory to You. In Jesus' name I pray. Amen.

Day 27

Acts 17:28 *For in Him we live and move and have our being. As some of your own poets have said, "We are His offspring."*

It is God who enables us to live, to move and to have our being and as your baby begins to have life, to move and to be, God provides him (her) with the placenta which enables him (her) to live and to move as it provides nutrients and oxygen. As the embryo develops it needs more and more nourishment from you which he (she) receives via the placenta. The placenta also serves as a filter to protect the embryo from dangerous substances in your blood. This filter, known as the placental barrier keeps many drugs from entering into the embryo. But it does not protect against all drugs, which can cause fetal damage if they enter the embryo in large quantities. This is why it is very important to consult a doctor before taking any medication during pregnancy.

Lord, I thank You for creating a baby to live and to move within me. As my baby grows, I pray that he (she) would receive all of the nutrients and oxygen that is needed to thrive. Please enable the placenta to form a strong barrier that protects the baby from any damaging drugs. I ask that You would keep me healthy during my pregnancy so that I would not have to take any medication. If I do become sick, I pray that the doctors will be able to prescribe medicine for me that will not damage my baby. In Jesus' name I pray. Amen.

Day 28

Colossians 1:16-17 *For by Him all things were created, things in Heaven and on earth, visible and invisible, whether thrones or powers or rulers or authorities; all things were created by Him and for Him. He is before all things and in Him all things hold together.*

The Lord holds all things together because He has created all things both here on earth and in Heaven. This holds true for your baby as well, for God has created an umbilical cord to hold the placenta and embryo together. This cord is made up of three blood vessels. One large one brings oxygenated blood and nutrients to the embryo and the other two remove the deoxygenated blood and its waste products from the embryo to the placenta. Even though this exchange takes place very quickly, it is essential for the life of the embryo.

Lord, You have created all things and are the binding agent that holds all things together. I praise You for designing and creating my baby's umbilical cord which enables the embryo and the placenta to be held together in the womb. I ask that You would give my baby a strong and well-functioning umbilical cord so that he (she) would be able to easily receive all the oxygen and nutrients that he (she) needs and that his (her) waste products would be removed without any problems. Lord, I also ask that You would protect my baby from becoming entangled in the umbilical cord. In Jesus' name I pray. Amen.

Day 29

1 Timothy 4:4 *For everything God created is good and nothing is to be rejected if it is received with thanksgiving.*

There are many verses in the Bible that speak against the act of abortion and I believe that this is one of the strongest. God instructs us through Paul's letter to Timothy that everything He creates is good. If you find out that your child may be born with a disability or a deformity, you may be overwhelmed with grief, with many thoughts running through your mind. You may often question why God would do this. This situation came up in the Gospel of John. Jesus' disciples asked him, upon seeing a blind man, *"Rabbi, who sinned, this man or his parents that he was born blind?"* Jesus replied, *"Neither this man or his parents sinned, but this happened so that the work of God may be displayed in his life."* And with this Jesus healed the blind man (John 9:1-3). This passage may not make bad news easier to accept, but it may explain why God gives us difficulties in our lives. Each time we experience troubles and look to God for relief, we are growing closer to Him and are glorifying Him with our lives.

Lord, I pray that my baby would be born having perfect health. I ask that as You mold and make this child he (she) would be free from all deformities and diseases. However, if it is Your plan to create him (her) with special needs, I pray that I would accept this with the attitude of Christ and that I would have the strength to provide my child with all he (she) might need. Please help me to accept this child as Your own, created in Your image as good to glorify You. In Jesus' name I pray. Amen.

Day 30

Revelation 4:11 *You are worthy, Our Lord and God to receive glory and honor and power, for You created all things and by Your will they were created and have their being.*

As I close this chapter on life, I am beyond convinced that God is the true Author of Life. When you become pregnant it is God that gives your baby life. He brings the egg to the point of ovulation and enables the sperm to be strong enough to penetrate the egg. It is the Lord who creates each cell, bringing each organ, muscle and bone into existence. He gives the baby a placenta and an umbilical cord to ensure its supply of oxygen and nutrients as he or she grows within you for forty weeks. Many biblical events were subject to the number forty. Noah spent forty days on the ark, Moses spent forty years in the desert, Jesus spent forty days fasting in the wilderness and your baby will spend forty weeks growing inside you, maturing under God's provision and His timing.

Lord, You have created all things. Everything that exists does so because of You. I thank You for creating my child and giving him (her) life. I pray that he (she) will grow under Your sovereignty and develop in accordance with Your will. Please bless this baby's health. I also ask that as he (she) grows into a strong, vigorous child throughout his (her) life here on earth, he (she) would use the body that You have so graciously given him (her) to bring You glory and honor. In Jesus' name I pray. Amen.

Month 3:
The Promise of Growth

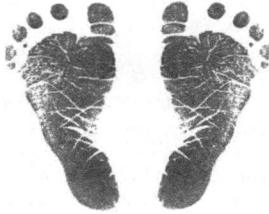

Day 1

Job 10:8 *Your hands shaped and made me.*

As God's hand shapes and makes your baby, perhaps the organ that is most remarkable to scientists is the brain. The brain is composed of cells that can react to impulses as well as analyze and control behavior and at just seven weeks of life, your baby's brain has nerve cells that begin to touch one another and have even become connected in primitive nerve paths. As your baby continues to grow, 100,000 new nerve cells are created every minute so that by the time he (she) is born, he (she) will have close to 100 billion nerve cells.

Lord, I praise You for using Your hands to shape and make my child. Only You can create him (her) in Your perfect way. As this baby grows within me, his (her) brain is being formed. Without a brain, he (she) would be in a vegetative state. But You have designed my child to be a rational, thinking creature and I pray that You would give him (her) a brain that allows him (her) to do just that. Please ensure that his (her) nerve cells will be connected properly and that the correct amount of nerve cells will be formed in his (her) brain. I ask that he (she) would be free from all brain damage and that his (her) brain would be his (her) most valued body part. In Jesus' name I pray. Amen.

Day 2

Psalm 1:3 *He is like a tree planted by streams of water, which yields its fruit in due season and whose leaf does not whither.*

Just as a tree planted by streams of water grows strong under God's guidance, by the time your baby is eight weeks old, he (she) will have developed each of the organs that he (she) will have at the time of birth. Even though the baby is only four centimeters in size, he (she) contains all that is needed to keep from "withering" at birth. Once these organs, such as the heart and brain have been formed, the risk of malformations decreases as does the danger for miscarriage. Scientists and doctors now graduate the term for the baby from embryo to fetus. Most of the design work is complete and the baby must now concentrate on the growth and development of each of these parts.

Lord, I praise You for the way that You maintain life. You will enable my baby to flourish just as You provide for the growth of a tree. As my pregnancy progresses into its forth month, You have ensured that each of his (her) organs are formed. Please enable the baby to grow and develop so that he (she) will be fruitful and will not wither. I pray that You would protect the baby from any malformations and that I would not suffer the loss of a miscarriage. In Jesus' name I pray. Amen.

Day 3

Psalm 52:8a *But I am like an olive tree flourishing in the house of God.*

Under God's sovereignty, your baby will flourish just as an olive tree does in the house of God. Your baby started out as one cell and from that cell, has developed many more, each one with a specific task that has been previously programmed. And the mystery that this development leaves for scientists proves the role that God plays in the baby's flourishing. The questions that we could ask, "How does this cell know that it is to be the lens of the eye while another cell knows that it will be part of the retina?" cannot be specifically answered by science because they are under God's control. God has told each cell what to become, which genes it should employ and which to exclude. The development of human babies follows a pattern that was determined by God at the beginning of history.

Lord, I praise You for enabling my baby to flourish just as an olive tree grown in Your house does. I know that as humans we try to wrap our minds around every aspect of life but I also know what we are not capable of understanding life as You do. You developed my baby's pattern of growth and You are the one that tells his (her) cells what to become and how to develop. I pray to You now asking that I would be at peace with the fetal growth process and that I would trust You to bring about my baby's growth in a way that enables him (her) to flourish in his (her) life here on Earth. In Jesus' name I pray. Amen.

Day 4

Psalm 92:12-13 *The righteousness will flourish like a palm tree, they will grow like a cedar of Lebanon; planted in the house of the Lord. They will flourish in the courts of our God.*

There are many times where God compares the development of a tree with that of humans. I believe that He uses this simile to show that even though trees are much less important to God than we are, He causes them to grow and blossom and He will do at least that much for us and our children. A tree needs sunlight, soil and water to grow. As long as God provides the perfect amount of each of these, it will grow in abundance with leaves and fruit. The signs of a flourishing baby look much different than that of a tree. But in the same way that a tree depends on God's control for ample but not overwhelming amounts of sunlight, water and soil to blossom, your unborn baby depends on God to provide him (her) with the proper growth and cell development that he (she) needs to grow into a perfectly formed child.

Lord, I know that my baby is more valuable to You than any tree, be it palm or cedar. You will cause trees to flourish in Your house just as You enable my baby to grow inside me. I offer my baby to You today. Even though he (she) cannot live in Your courts just yet, while he (she) lives here with me on earth, I ask that my baby would receive Your provisions for his (her) flourishing. Help this baby to grow into the child that You have created him (her) to be. In Jesus' name I pray. Amen.

Day 5

Psalm 100:3 *Know that the Lord is God. It is He who made us and we are His people, the sheep of His pasture.*

God created us in all His sovereignty and He made us to be His people. He often refers to us as sheep, putting Himself in the role of shepherd. As a shepherd, it is His responsibility to care for the sheep, making sure that they grow and flourish. Likewise, it is God who cares for you and your baby, ensuring that he (she) develops inside you. Initially the embryo needed a yolk sac to form stem cells and white blood cells. But as God provides for the baby to grow to the eleventh week, the yolk sac has ceased to serve its purpose and the liver and the spleen begin to form the baby's blood cells. Also, the fetus's bone marrow starts to produce its own blood cells.

Lord, I rejoice in knowing that You are my shepherd and I ask that You would also watch over my child, keeping him (her) safe and strong in these stages of development. I praise You for the job that the yolk sac has done for my child, ensuring that he (she) had proper blood cells. I ask that now as his (her) tiny liver and spleen begin to create their own blood cells, along with the white blood cells created in his (her) bone marrow, that they would be successful in their production. Please ensure that throughout his (her) life he (she) has healthy blood cells and white blood cell count. In Jesus' name I pray. Amen.

Day 6

Psalm 103:13-14 *As a father has compassion on his children, so the Lord has compassion on those who fear Him; for He knows how we are formed, He remembers that we are dust.*

When God formed the first human being, He made him from the dust of the earth. In Ecclesiastes 3:20 it is written, *all come from dust, and to dust all return.* This popular Bible verse speaks of the inevitability of death and at the same time of the fragility of human life. It gives credit to our Creator who breathed life into dust and at the same time makes us humble knowing that in His time our bodies will return to the dust from which they were created. God has formed your baby to have the same fragility in his (her) life. The certainty of knowing that one day God will call him (her) home and the uncertainty of knowing when is one of life's greatest dichotomies. It always makes me turn to God and seek His sovereignty in my life.

Lord, I know that You are the great Creator. You dreamed us up and gave us life. We are created with the dust of the ground and Your very own breath. This gives us both royal and humble origins. We know that we belong to You and that You have called us to share in Your inheritance. But at the same time, we can grow comfortable with our lives here, not wanting to surrender to the unknown of death. Lord, I praise You for giving life to my baby, for forming him (her) out of dust. And it seems strange to be praying about his (her) death even before he (she) has taken his (her) first breath, but he (she) is human and I know that one day his (her) body will return to dust. I ask that if I am still alive when that happens, I would be able to trust in Your plan, knowing that he (she) is in Your care. Please help my child to accept Your plan of salvation as soon as possible so that he (she) can surely be counted among those residing in heaven. I also ask that You make this transition as peaceful as possible for both him (her) and those close to him (her). In Jesus' name I pray. Amen.

Day 7

Psalm 115:14 *May the Lord make you increase both you and your children.*

It is God's plan for us to increase. This verse speaks of the role of families and how it is God's plan for us to have children and grandchildren in our lives. God desires for us to have many descendents and this is one way that He blesses us during our lives on earth. For although children are not easy to raise, there is nothing that can bring us the same joy that they enable us to feel. When I took a closer look at this verse, I also saw that the word increase could have another meaning. One of the most blessed ways we can increase is through spiritual growth and a greater love for God. As we increase our love for God, we will find ourselves to be truly blessed as well.

Lord, I praise You for giving me the desire to increase myself with children and the ability and means to make that family come into existence. I pray that I would always be surrounded by a family of children and grandchildren. I also ask that You would increase the desire that I have for You in my heart. I want to know You better and to love You more. I believe that this kind of increase will truly enable me to live a life that is blessed by You. Lord, I also ask that You would increase my child's love for You as well. You have given each of us a measure of faith and I ask that You would take my child's portion and multiply it, giving him (her) a life that is increased in its closeness to You. In Jesus' name I pray. Amen.

Day 8

Psalm 138:8 *The Lord will fulfill His purpose for me.*

The Lord has created your child with a purpose in mind. We have looked closely at His promise of a plan in the last chapter and this verse serves as a reminder that as He gives life and ensures growth, each is taking place as a fulfillment of His will. Through each day and week that this baby is growing inside you, he (she) is developing into the person that God has called him (her) to be. Each step of the growth process brings him (her) closer to fulfilling God's plan for his (her) life. Your child does not exist apart from God's purpose for him (her). As you learn about the growth process and wonder how your unborn child is faring, it will calm you to know that the growth of the baby is taking place outside of your control, but very much inside God's control.

Lord, I know that besides living a healthy lifestyle, I have little control over the growth process of my baby. It is You who has brought him (her) to life and who causes him (her) to grow. You develop each cell, each organ, each bone. And as my baby develops inside me, I pray that I would be able to trust Your sovereignty. Please help me to see that You do nothing that is outside of Your perfect will. Show me that You have a purpose for my baby and help me to feel secure knowing that Your specific purpose for his (her) life will be fulfilled. In Jesus' name I pray. Amen.

Day 9

Psalm 139:9 *For You created my inmost being; You knit me together in my mother's womb.*

As your baby is being knit together in the womb, at about 11 weeks, he (she) starts to develop a face. It is this little face that you will first look at after delivery, searching for resemblances and standing (or laying) in awe of what God has created within you. To form the face, five outgrowths emerge and join under the skin of the fetus. The first will form the nose and the upper lip and the last will grow under the mouth, fusing to form the lower lip and chin. After the face is formed, muscles can then be attached to the base, enabling the face to move. The fetus can now make faces at you, including frowning, opening and closing the lips and turning the head.

Lord, I pray that You would bless the formation of my baby's face. The appearance that You will give this child will affect many aspects of his or her life. I pray that You would give him (her) a face that reflects the joy that he (she) will have for You within his (her) heart. Lord, You told Moses to bless the Israelites saying, "The Lord bless you and keep you; the Lord make his face shine upon you and be gracious to you; the Lord turn his face to you and give you peace" (Numbers 6:25). I pray this same blessing for my baby today. I ask that You would bless him (her) and keep him (her) and that You would make Your face shine upon him (her). Lord, please turn Your face to my baby and give him (her) peace. In Jesus' name I pray. Amen.

Day 10

Psalm 139:14 *I praise You because I am fearfully and wonderfully made; Your works are wonderful I know that full well.*

God has wonderfully created the baby within you. The work He is doing in your womb is both fearful and wonderful. The development of your baby's eyes is a remarkable example of God's making. When the eyes begin to form, the forebrain issues a hollow stalk on either side of the face. As the end of the stalk thickens, it forms a small sphere. When the sphere meets the inside of the skin, it turns inward on itself like a cup. The base of the cup becomes the back of the eyeball and the skin surface covering it becomes the retina. Inside the cup, the skin cells then form a lens and a cornea. On the front of the lens an iris grows inward from the edges. Finally, the surrounding skin folds over to form two eyelids. The eye is then complete.

Lord, I pray for the formation of my baby's eyes. I ask that he (she) would have perfect vision. Please bless the growth of his (her) eyes. Let the cells each form the parts of the eye that they are supposed to form. Please give him (her) retinas, lenses, irises and corneas that are perfectly healthy. Lord, You have created this world to possess much beauty. I pray that You would give my baby the ability to experience that beauty through sight. If he (she) does have vision problems, I pray that we could either have them corrected or make provisions so that he (she) can experience Your beauty through another means. In Jesus' name I pray. Amen.

Day 11

Psalm 139:15 *My frame was not hidden from You when I was formed in the secret place. When I was woven together in the depths of the earth.*

After eight weeks of being "woven together" the outer ear of the baby begins to take shape. However, it isn't until about the fifth month that it resembles a fully formed ear. It is also about this time that the baby begins to react to sounds. When the ear is being formed, it takes three directions. It begins with two hollows formed on either side of the brain, forming the inner ear which contains the auditory and balance organs. A little later, the outer ear develops containing the auditory canal and the outer side of the eardrum. The middle ear with auditory bones (hammer, anvil and stirrup) develops as a bulge from the pharynx. Each of these three parts works together to allow the baby to start hearing, even inside the womb. Singing or talking to your unborn baby may stimulate him (her) and help him (her) to recognize his (her) parents' voices.

Lord, I praise You for weaving my baby together inside my womb. You are the first one to know him (her) because You have created him (her). Lord, as You form this baby in this secret place, I pray that he (she) will have perfectly developed ears. I ask that he (she) will be able to hear without any problems. Please protect my baby as his (her) ears are being formed. I pray that I would have no illness that would cause malformations or hearing impairment in my baby. Please bless the development of his (her) inner, outer and middle ears and let them work together in perfect order. In Jesus' name I pray. Amen.

Day 12

Isaiah 29:22 *"No longer will Jacob be ashamed; no longer will their faces grow pale, when they see among them their children, the work of my hands, they will keep my name holy, they will acknowledge the holiness of the Holy One of Jacob and will stand in awe of the God of Israel."*

As God speaks through the prophet Isaiah, He tells His people that He is the one who gives them children. Our children are gifts from Him and are the work of His hands. When God gives us the gift of a child, He expects that we will have a certain reaction: keeping His name holy, acknowledging His holiness and standing in awe of Him. Without specifically knowing that this is what God expects of us, this is a natural reaction to the birth of a child. When I look at my child's face, I can not help but to acknowledge God's holiness and the work that He has done in my life. I am taken back by the awe I feel for a God that is so wonderful. As a woman who has conceived, carried and borne a child I do not know how there can be a woman who has gone through the same experience and not acknowledge the holiness of God.

Lord, I praise You for the child that You have created in me as a great gift from You. I thank You so much for the life within me and I ask that You would protect him (her) as he (she) grows and develops. I thank You for this gift of a child that evokes me to keep Your name holy, acknowledge Your holiness and stand in awe of You. In Jesus' name I pray. Amen.

Day 13

Isaiah 44:24 *This is what the Lord says, your Redeemer, who formed you in the womb, "I am the Lord, who has made all things."*

About five weeks after the Lord forms your baby in the womb, four small buds protrude from either side of the embryo. These buds look like small flippers. Two buds will soon create upper arms, forearms and hands and the other two will be the thighs, lower legs and feet. The hands are formed before the feet and then the arms and legs become elongated. By the third or fourth month the hands can grasp and the feet can kick but the movements are too weak to be felt at this point.

Lord, You are the maker of all things. As You form my baby in the womb I pray that he (she) would have perfectly developed arms and legs. Please give him (her) forearms and hands, thighs and feet that would work together. I ask that he (she) would have perfectly working ligaments, muscles and joints. Please keep him (her) from suffering from multiple sclerosis or muscular dystrophy or any other disease. Give this baby strong bones and protect him (her) from any injuries. I pray that my child would be able to use these body parts to bring honor and praise to Your name. In Jesus' name I pray. Amen.

Day 14

Isaiah 49:2 *He made my mouth like a sharpened sword, in the shadow of His hand He hid me; He made me into a polished arrow and concealed me in His quiver.*

When the Lord creates a child, He does so according to His own will. He designs His children to perfectly fulfill His plan. The prophet Isaiah compares this perfection to a sharpened sword and a polished arrow. As His perfect creation, God also protects us. He hides us from danger in His hand and conceals us in His "quiver" so that we can have the freedom to serve His purpose. The sword and the arrow are very valuable tools to a hunter or a soldier. They help him maintain and achieve life through power and protection. In a similar way, when we use the tools and abilities that God has given us through our minds and bodies, we become valuable members of God's army, winning souls and spiritual battles in God's name.

Lord, I praise You for the perfection that You put into the creation of my baby. I know that no matter how much I love him (her), he (she) is even more valuable to You for he (she) is also Your child. I ask that as my baby is formed, his (her) mouth would be like a sharpened sword and that You would make him (her) into a polished arrow. I pray that You would also give him (her) Your protection in this world. Lord, please hide my child in Your hand and conceal him (her) in Your quiver so that he (she) would be protected from evil. And Lord, I ask that my child would choose to use the body that You have given him (her) to glorify and serve You throughout his (her) life. In Jesus' name I pray. Amen.

Day 15

Isaiah 49:3 *He said to me, "You are my servant, Israel, in whom I will display my splendor.*

God displays His splendor in each child that He creates. One of the ways that God's splendor is displayed is through the flexibility that He instills in the bones of unborn babies. Because the rate of growth and development is very fast for the fetus, his (her) structure cannot be made of bone, but rather is composed of cartilage that will eventually become bone. This initial structure is softer and more malleable than bone. This flexibility enables the baby's head to suffer indentations during delivery. Additionally, the birthing process may result in collarbones and upper arms breaking. However, because God has created the structure to be so soft, these injuries are healed spontaneously and swiftly.

Lord, I pray that as You are forming my baby, You would create him (her) to be Your servant. I ask that You would use him (her) as a means to display Your splendor. I praise You for creating my baby with cartilage so that he (she) would quickly heal from any injuries and I ask that this initial structure would convert to strong and healthy bones at the right time. I also ask that You would protect him (her) from all types of bone disease including bone cancer, osteoporosis, scoliosis, achondroplasia, myeloma, Paget's disease or any other bone diseases. In Jesus' name I pray. Amen.

Day 16

Isaiah 61:3 *They will be called oaks of righteousness, a planting of the Lord for the display of his splendor.*

As God creates babies to display His splendor, we know that He creates them in His own image. Additionally, every child models one of the first two humans, Adam and Eve. At the time of fertilization the sex of the baby has been determined to be either male or female. If the child is male, a small bud will develop between the legs and two swellings will emerge on either side of the bud that will grow together to form the scrotum. The process in a female is similar, however, the small bud will become a clitoris and a slit will develop between the two swellings to form a vagina. Interestingly enough, by about four months, the male fetus will have ducts of testicles with the precursors of sperm beginning to develop and the female will have ovaries that already contain the 5 million ova that they will produce in her lifetime.

Lord, I pray for the development of my child's sex organs. I ask that You would clearly delineate one sex for my baby and that the organs that belong to that sex would be in perfect working order. I never want my child to feel as if he (she) has been born with the wrong sex organs or that he (she) was really meant to be another sex. Please help this child to feel comfortable with the sex that You have chosen for him (her) and keep him (her) free from any sexual dysfunction. In Jesus' name I pray. Amen.

Day 17

Isaiah 64:8 *Yet O Lord, You are our Father. We are the clay, You are the potter; we are all the work of Your hand.*

God has created His children as the work of His hands. Just as a potter molds clay, God molds the cells within you to create a baby. As that baby grows to about eighteen weeks, you can begin to feel God's work moving inside you. This is such an incredible feeling. At first it's hard to tell what the feeling is because it's better experienced than described, but if I had to describe it I would say that it feels like bubbles popping inside you. Even though the fetus has been moving inside you for many weeks, your abdomen is now beginning to become slightly rounded and the movements are becoming strong enough to be felt through the abdominal wall.

Lord, there are many unpleasant aspects of pregnancy, nausea, exhaustion, weight gain, moodiness, and so on. However, one of the most pleasant experiences of carrying a child is being able to be the first one to feel the baby moving. Lord, I praise You for creating such an amazing feeling and for letting me experience it firsthand. Lord, please give my baby whatever he (she) needs to keep on moving for the next few months. In Jesus' name I pray. Amen.

Day 18

Jeremiah 12:2a *You have planted them and they have taken root.*

God plants your child within you and as the baby takes root inside your womb, you may experience a number of ailments associated with an enlarged uterus. The first of these is varicose veins. These veins are the result of the enlarged uterus pressing on large veins in the pelvis. This makes blood pressure in the veins higher than usual and causes them to swell. Avoiding long periods of standing may help but surgery may also be needed a few months after delivery to remove the veins. A second problem associated with the pressure that the enlarged uterus puts on the vein in the pelvis is hemorrhoids but these seldom need to be operated on and usually heal after delivery. A diet full of fruit, vegetables, whole grains and exercise can help avoid the straining of constipation that can bring on hemorrhoids.

Lord, I know that since the fall of man in the Garden of Eden, women have been subject to suffering during pregnancy and delivery. I ask that if my uterus does expand and put pressure on the veins in my pelvis, I would not suffer severely from varicose veins or hemorrhoids. Help me to stay off my feet as much as possible, to eat a healthy diet and to exercise. However, if my veins do swell and damage is done to the valves of my veins, I pray that this would quickly heal after the birth of my child, or that a simple surgery would be able to correct this. In Jesus' name I pray. Amen.

Day 19

Jeremiah 24:7 *"I will give them a heart to know me that I am the Lord."*

The heart is one of the most important organs in the body. At the center of the circulatory system, it pumps blood to every part of the body. This blood contains the oxygen and nutrients that every part of our body needs to function. The right side of the heart receives blood that is low in oxygen from the veins and pumps it to the lungs where it renews its oxygen supply and gets rid of any carbon dioxide. The left side of the heart then takes the "good" blood from the lungs and pumps it back into the veins. This muscle and the system it controls is what keeps the body alive. But the heart is much more than a muscle because it also represents our emotions. We "love" with our heart. When God forms our hearts, He intends for it to keep us alive by pumping blood, but He also wants the emotions of our heart to focus on Him. He has given us a heart so that we will know and love Him.

Lord, I pray again for my baby's heart. Please protect it as it is being formed and enable it to pump blood to every part of his (her) body, keeping a perfect balance of carbon dioxide and oxygen. Please protect my baby's heart from any disease. I ask that he (she) would be free from any congenital heart defects, arrhythmias, murmurs, high blood pressure, diabetes, or any other condition that would weaken his (her) heart. I do not want him (her) to have heart failure at any time. Let my baby have a strong heart and let it not only be a muscle in his (her) body, but also an organ that directs his (her) emotions to You. Please give my baby a heart that knows that You are the Lord and that loves You. In Jesus' name I pray. Amen.

Day 20

Ezekiel 16:6-7a *"I made you grow like a plant of the field, you grew up and developed and became the most beautiful of jewels."*

Through your eating, breathing and just plain living, your baby will grow inside you. The baby knows exactly what needs to be done in order to develop, however it doesn't really "do" anything. Nor do you. The growth process is one that happens, not on its own, but under the direction of God. God causes plants to grow in the field without any help or effort on the part of the plant and in the same way your baby will grow inside you and develop and "become the most beautiful of jewels."

Lord, I pray for the role You play in the development of my baby. It is You who causes everything to grow, including the life within me. I pray that as the plants in the fields grow without any effort, my baby too can rely totally on You for his (her) growth and development. Please enable him (her) to grow and develop to be a healthy child. I ask that You would keep him (her) free from all diseases and defects during his (her) life, for You are the great Protector. I know that my baby will be the most beautiful of jewels in my eyes but I also ask that he (she) would reflect the same beauty in his (her) love and commitment to You. In Jesus' name I pray. Amen.

Day 21

Ezekiel 19:10 *Your mother was like a vine in your vineyard, planted by the water; it was fruitful and full of branches because of abundant water.*

In the Lord's vineyard, water is abundant. There are no droughts and no deluges. The amount of sun and water are in perfect balance for the production of fruitful branches. A mother who is like a vine in the Lord's vineyard has found the perfect balance for rest and exercise during pregnancy. Any cardiovascular activities can be healthy in moderation. These can include swimming, tennis, hiking or aerobics or any other sport that does not involve contact. Pregnancy can put a heavy strain on the back because of all the extra weight that the mother carries in the front of the abdomen. Exercise will also create strong and mobile back muscles which can be an advantage during labor.

Lord, I want to be the type of mother who is like a vine in Your vineyard. I desire fruitful branches. Please help me to find a healthy balance of rest and exercise during this pregnancy. My body may experience exhaustion at times and when I feel tired, I pray that I will have the time to rest. I also ask that I will not become sedentary but will have the desire to engage in a healthy exercise routine. Please keep me from being injured during any exercise. I ask that nothing I would do would bring stress on my body or the baby within me. In Jesus' name I pray. Amen.

Day 22

Ezekiel 37:5-6 *This is what the Sovereign Lord says to these bones, "I will make breath enter you, and you will come to life. I will attach tendons to you and make flesh come upon you and cover you with skin. I will put breath in you and you will come to life. Then you will know that I am the Lord."*

Through the prophet Ezekiel, God again proclaims His role in the creation of life. God controls the cells within your baby that cause skin and bone to grow. He also attaches tendons and muscles to the bones so that they can move. God puts two little lungs in the chest of your baby so that when he (she) is delivered into the world he (she) can take his (her) first breath. We have looked at each of these stages of development, from the three layers of skin to the transformation of cartilage to bone. As your baby grows each day he (she) is becoming stronger and developing more into the child that God has called him (her) to be. The purpose of God's role in this process is to reveal to us that He is the Lord. As your baby grows more and more into the image of God, he (she) is living proof to the world, as much as to us, that He is the Lord.

Lord, I thank You for creating my baby and forming him (her) in Your perfect way. I ask You Lord to oversee his (her) development so that he (she) grows into a healthy child. Please give this child skin that is free from any diseases and bones and muscles that successfully serve their purpose. Lord, I pray that my baby will have two perfect lungs that will enable him (her) to easily breathe the air that You have provided. Please give him (her) a body that will receive the breath that You give so that he (she) will not only come to life in this world, but will also live a long, healthy life, worshiping and serving You. In Jesus' name I pray. Amen.

Day 23

Malachi 2:10a *Have we not all one Father? Did not one God create us?*

As the fetus grows, it puts on weight by creating a protective layer of fat in its dermis. While the baby is putting on weight, it is important that you do not gain too much weight. Again, it is best to find a healthy balance. Too much weight gain will give the baby an excess supply of fat at birth and may make delivery more complicated. Inadequate eating may leave either the baby or you malnourished. This can be detrimental to the foundations of the brain functions that are formed before the baby is born. At birth, the baby's brain has hundreds of billions of nerve cells which are formed and developed in the prenatal stage. It is believed that after birth, no new nerve cells arise. It is therefore important that healthy brain cells are maintained during our entire lives and having a diet that is high in nutrition will enable you to give your baby the best start.

Lord, You are the Father of all of us, and I praise You for creating my baby. I pray for my diet during my pregnancy. I pray that my baby and I would have a healthy weight gain during this time. I do not want him (her) to gain too much weight, nor do I want him (her) to be malnourished. I pray also for my baby's nerve cells. While he (she) is a fetus, he (she) will undergo the formation of many nerve cells that will control his (her) brain functions. I pray that these cells would be ample in number and strong in composition. In Jesus' name I pray. Amen.

Day 24

Luke 2:40 *And the child grew and became strong; He was filled with wisdom and the grace of God was upon Him.*

Jesus, the Son of God, came to life in human form so that He could provide the ultimate sacrifice for the sins of the world. As a human, He experienced everything that we experience, both the emotional and the physical. And as a child, He went through the same growth process that our children do. One difference was His beginning. He was not conceived by a male's sperm penetrating a woman's egg. His life began with the Holy Spirit entering the body of a virgin named Mary. How much of His development from that point is different from any other human is known only by God. But we do know that He grew and developed inside Mary's womb and as a child in her care.

Lord, I praise and thank You for the gift You have given each of us in the life of Your Son. Through His death and resurrection we have been promised eternal life. I also thank You for the example that Jesus' life gives to each of us. Through His humanity we can experience first hand what it means to live a sinless life. I ask that You would enable my baby to grow and become strong, both in my womb and then in the world, just as Your Son did so many years ago. I also ask that like Jesus, he (she) would be filled with wisdom and that Your grace would be upon him (her). In Jesus' name I pray. Amen.

Day 25

Luke 2:51-52 *Then He went down to Nazareth with them and was obedient to them. But His mother treasured all these things in her heart. And Jesus grew in wisdom and stature, and in favor with God and men.*

Mary is such a great example for us. We admire her because God chose her to be the mother of his Son, so she must have had unique qualities. But at the same time, she was human and experienced all of the same emotions as a mother that we do. She treasured her son, not just because he was the Son of God, but because He was her son, and as she was able to see her son grow and develop, she felt the pleasure that any mother would. I'm sure that He brought her much joy in His youth as she experienced the satisfaction of raising a son. Jesus may have been easier to raise than most children due to His sinless nature, but nonetheless caring for a child and a household would have brought Mary to experience the spectrum of motherly emotions. And although we do not know many details about Mary's experience in motherhood, we can assume that whatever qualities she possessed to be chosen as the mother of God would be expressed in her daily life.

Lord, I know that the only perfect human in the world was Your Son Jesus Christ. However, His mother Mary must have been a special woman for You to choose her out of all the women in the world to be the mother of Your Son. Mary did not have the easiest of situations. She gave birth alone, in a cave where animals were kept. She lived during a time that was not privy to microwave ovens or disposable diapers and still, she successfully raised the Son of God. Lord, please give me a little of the strength that she had. Please help me to treasure my baby at all times and enable him (her) to grow in wisdom and stature. I want this child to find favor with both You and the people of this world. In Jesus' name I pray. Amen.

Day 26

1 Corinthians 3:6 *I planted the seed, Apollos watered it, but God made it grow.*

As mothers we are servants of God. As we find ourselves selflessly giving to our children and families, we are obeying God's plan for us. We can take care of our children's physical needs by feeding them, bathing them and caring for them in general. We can also care for their emotional needs by giving them lots of hugs, praise, support and even discipline. But it is also our responsibility to provide for their spiritual needs. Through our example and teaching we can "plant" and "water" the seeds of Christ in their lives. We can read them Bible stories, sing Christian songs to them and teach them how to pray. If your child grows into a strong adult then he (she) will have a healthy body. If he (she) is emotionally sound then he (she) will have a healthy mind. But if he (she) walks and grows with God then he (she) will have a healthy soul and an eternal life in heaven with the Lord.

Lord, I thank You for my role as a mother. Even though there are moments when I am tired of my daily chores and stressed out by the wiles of a child, I know that by being this baby's mother I am serving You. Every diaper I change and every meal I serve is done as a means of doing Your will. Lord, please help me not only to care for my child's body, but his (her) mind and spirit as well. Show me how to plant and water the seeds of Christ's love so that my child will grow to know and love You. I ask that he (she) would have a strong body and a sound mind, but most of all I desire that he (she) would walk in Your will and grow daily in service and love for You. In Jesus' name I pray. Amen.

Day 27

1 Corinthians 3:7 *So neither he who plants nor he who waters is anything, but only God who makes things grow.*

These verses in First Corinthians speak of divisions in and among churches. At the time that the apostles were spreading the gospel, people, in their "worldliness" tried to say that whoever they followed was better than the others. This brought about jealousy and quarrelling. Paul, knowing that God desired unity, wrote to the church of Corinth and told them that he and his friends were all servants of God and that one was not superior to another, because it was God who was really working within them. I equate this analogy of growth with that of a child. As your child grows physically within you, you can look to God for His provision of growth. It is God that causes everything to grow. And as our children grow in the world, it is our job as parents to see to their spiritual growth. We are to serve God by finding as many opportunities as possible to bring our children closer to Jesus.

Lord, I thank You for the servants who have spread Your gospel throughout the ages. It is their hard work and struggles that have provided for the spiritual growth of so many of Your followers. I know that I may not have the responsibility of creating or leading a church, but You have put me in charge of this precious child and I seek Your guidance and wisdom as I raise him (her) to be a follower of You. Help me to show my baby how to pray and give him (her) a large gift of faith so that his (her) love for and obedience to You will be unshakeable. Please help me to mold him (her) to be one of Your many servants and give him (her) the desire to know You better and to love You more with each day of his (her) life. In Jesus' name I pray. Amen.

Day 28

1 Corinthians 3:9 *For we are God's fellow workers; you are God's field, God's building.*

Usually the word "church" invokes visions of a building. It may be a fancy building with many stained glass windows or a plain one with little fanfare. However, church is not necessarily a place to go but is, and has always been a group of people that come together to worship and learn about God. It is the people that make up the "field" and the "building" of God. As we meet with fellow Christians, we may have different roles of service within the church, some greater than others. But as mothers, we each have a special "field" in which to work and that is in the hearts and minds of our children. So many times we can get wrapped up in the "important" tasks of serving the "church" that we may neglect the ones we are called to serve in our own house. This is not a call to give up any church service, because if your church is anything like mine, you play a vital part, but please ensure that your children do not feel neglected as a result of your service to others.

Lord, I thank You for the "field" you have given me. You have entrusted me with a part of Your kingdom. Each one of us has different talents and responsibilities, but as a mother, I know that at least part of my "field" is made up of my children. Please help me see to it that I am a faithful servant of the work You have set before me, for You have said in Matthew 25, that he who can be trusted with little can be trusted with much and he who can not be trusted with little can not be trusted with much. You have entrusted me with the responsibility of sharing Christ with this child and I pray that I make this a priority in my life. In Jesus' name I pray. Amen.

Day 29

1 Corinthians 12:18 *But in fact God has arranged the parts of the body, every one of them, just as He wanted them to be.*

This chapter has been focused around the physical, emotional and spiritual growth of our children. Through it, we have seen how God is the source of all growth. He has designed the human body with many parts, all performing separate jobs but working together to give life and function to the body. The body is also a metaphor for the body of Christ, for as members of a church, we each have different responsibilities, none more important than the other, all working together to serve God. God has designed your child's body with each part just as He wanted it to be. It is through His provision that your child will develop each part and together, his (her) body will be perfectly formed and ready to serve God in whatever way God has prepared for him (her).

Lord, I praise You for the perfect design of the human body. And although I may find many flaws with mine, especially through aging and post-pregnancy, I know that I was designed in Your image and pray that I will use my body to glorify You. Lord, I also pray for the design and development of my baby's body. Please arrange each part just as You want it to be. Give each part of his (her) body the ability to perform the function for which it was formed and enable this child to use his (her) body to bring glory to Your name. In Jesus' name I pray. Amen.

Day 30

1 Peter 2:2 *Like newborn babies crave pure, spiritual milk, so that by it you may grow up in your salvation now that you have tasted that the Lord is good.*

Once we accept God's plan of salvation, we have only taken an initial step in our walk with Him. God wants us to crave the continuance of a spiritual walk with Him just as babies crave milk from their mothers. When your baby comes into the world, you can choose to feed him (her) with bottles and formula, or breast milk or some combination of the two. The process of breastfeeding begins with a reflex to the baby's sucking. A nerve reflex from the nipples reaches certain centers in the lower portion of the brain, causing the pituitary gland to secrete the hormone prolactin, which is needed for milk production. Another hormone from the pituitary gland simultaneously affects the milk glands and ducts which causes the milk to be squeezed out of the breast. Initially the breasts produce colostrum, which is a special, thick milk that is low in fat, high in protein and is extremely easy for the baby to digest. After a few days of breastfeeding, the standard breast milk will begin to flow.

Lord, I pray that You would guide me in the way that I choose to feed my baby. Please show me what is best for this child and our situation and let me not be pressured by outside opinions. If I do choose to breastfeed, I pray that my baby will not have a hard time latching on to my breast. Please give him (her) a good appetite so that he (she) can eat abundantly and feel satisfied. I pray that my breasts will not become too sore and that the milk I produce would be the perfect food for my child. Please keep me free from any illness that would prevent me from nursing. I pray that my husband and family would be supportive of whatever means I choose to feed my child and that this decision would be a natural one, without any added stress. In Jesus' name I pray. Amen.

Month 4:
The Promise of a Plan

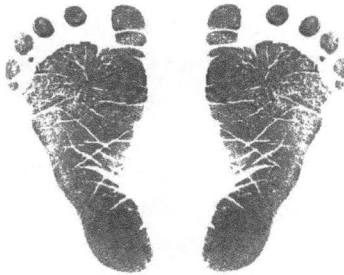

Day 1

Exodus 9:16 *"But I have raised you up for this very purpose, that I may show you my power and that my name might be proclaimed in all the earth."*

This verse was spoken by Moses to Pharaoh as a message from God as Moses was pleading for the freedom of the Israelite people. God told Pharaoh that He had raised him up for a purpose which was to use him as a way to exhibit God's power and proclaim His name. This purpose does not just have to be for someone as powerful as Pharaoh. It can be for us and for our children as well. God can and wants to use each of His children to exhibit His power and to proclaim His name. All we have to do is ask for these opportunities and be prepared for amazing things to happen.

Lord, I ask that You would use my child to fulfill the purposes You have for his (her) life. Please give him (her) many opportunities to exhibit Your power and proclaim Your name. Show my baby Your supreme authority so that he (she) may testify to others of the work You have done in his (her) life. Give him (her) the opportunity and courage to proclaim Your name to as many people as You desire. Let his (her) vision of You be strong and unclouded and let the words of profession come easily from his (her) mouth. Please give him (her) the courage to speak and the wisdom to chose the perfect words. In Jesus name I pray. Amen.

Day 2

Job 36:5 *God is mighty, but does not despise men; He is mighty and firm in His purpose.*

God is mighty. Might, is defined in the dictionary as "great or superior strength, power, force or vigor." This great and superior strength is made available to us through God. In the most desperate moments of my life I have looked to God to give me just an ounce of His strength or His peace or whatever I need to overcome my adversity and He has proved to be faithful. God does not despise us, conversely, He loves us and has made our lives part of His firm purpose. We can have peace in our lives knowing that His purpose is mighty.

Lord, I praise You for Your strength and might. Thank You for loving me and making me a part of Your firm purpose. I pray that my child will quickly learn Your love. Please let the love that I have for him (her) be the perfect model for the way You love him (her). I want my baby to know that even though I love him (her) as much as I can, Your love for him (her) supersedes my human love. Please make Your purposes for his (her) life evident to us so we can rest in Your might. In Jesus' name I pray. Amen.

Day 3

Job 42:2 *I know that You can do all things, no plan of Yours can be thwarted.*

If anyone had a right to doubt God it could have been Job. God allowed this follower to be put through the greatest of tests, including the loss of his family. But Job withstood Satan, knowing that God will prevail. If I could only maintain a touch of Job's faith my life would have much fewer worries. Job knew about God's power. He knew that Satan could not overcome God's plan for his life. And if he had to go through some drama to demonstrate his faith in God, he did so with confidence in God's power.

Lord, Your will cannot be thwarted. When You assign a plan to our lives it will be fulfilled. You are a strong and awesome God who has shown Your power throughout the history of time as much as through the history of my life. Please use this power to fulfill the plans You have for my child's life. Give him (her) a strong belief in You that enables him (her) to demonstrate his (her) faith even through the drama of his (her) life. If You do allow Satan to tempt him (her), please give my child the strength to look to You and act in obedience of Your word. In Jesus' name I pray. Amen.

Day 4

Psalm 20:4 *May He give You the desire of Your heart and make all Your plans succeed.*

When we pray for agreement between our plans and God's will, we will hopefully eliminate the frustration we may feel when our plans are obstructed because they are not aligned with God's will. We can then pray that God will fulfill the desires of our hearts and that our plans will succeed. When our plans and God's plans coincide, their chances of succeeding are 100%. The only way to ensure that what we want to happen in our lives will come to be is to seek the guidance of the Holy Spirit so that our plans to walk and our actual walk will be directed by God.

Lord, I pray that You will give me the desires of my heart during this pregnancy. I ask that the Holy Spirit would fill my mind as I make plans for this child so that those plans would succeed. Lord, my strongest desire is for a healthy child and a safe delivery. I ask that there would be no complications during the birth process and I desire that my child would be a strong baby, vigorous and vibrant in life. These are the plans that I have for my child and I now ask that they would be aligned with Your will so that their success would be secured. In Jesus' name I pray. Amen.

Day 5

Psalm 33:11 *The plans of the Lord stand firm forever, the purposes of His heart through all generations.*

The Lord's plans are stronger than all other plans. They are the ones that will prevail. What is also true, as this verse points out, is that the plans of God are also strong against time. Sometimes I might plan to do something and it doesn't come to be. Something else may come up, situations may change, priorities may get realigned or I just might not get around to it. Whatever the case, I might put it off until a later time, or forget it altogether. As a human, my plans are feeble but God's plans are strong. The plans that he has for us are everlasting. They were not just true for the people of Abraham's time, or David's or Jesus'. They are true of every generation and of every child of God including you and your baby.

Lord, the purposes of Your heart have stood firm for all of time. Your plans have been executed in Your perfect time, especially the plans made true in Your son. He is the ultimate fulfillment of all You purposed and spoke of in the Old Testament. He came to fulfill the prophesy that You gave so many years before His reign on earth. There is no better evidence of the strength of Your plans and I praise You for this. I ask that You would strengthen the plans for my child's life. Please set Your purposes in his (her) heart so his (her) life would be a testament to Your power. In Jesus' name I pray. Amen.

Day 6

Psalm 40:5 *Many, O Lord, my God are the wonders You have done. The things You planned for us no one can recount to You; were I to speak and tell of them, they would be too many to declare.*

We make plans, set goals, and have lists and deadlines. We may outline what we want to accomplish with our lives from the ten year plan to the shopping list for the food store. These plans keep our work and our lives organized. As a teacher, my lesson plan book is one of my most valuable possessions. I'm constantly planning and re-planning, and when I look back in June, I can see all the work I've done. However, there is no one who can recount the plans of God. He has so much in store for our lives. He has brought us to where we are today, perhaps with one of life's best plans, the plan to be a parent. Just as my lesson plan book has some great lessons and some not so great lessons in it, our lives may sometimes seem to take on a roller coaster effect. But when we look at the plans and purpose of our lives as declared by God, we can be confident that they are never out of His control.

Lord, I know You have planned my child's life even before one of its days has begun. You know this baby's hair color, eye color, how tall he (she) will be, the jobs he (she) will have, his (her) happiness and sadness. Every detail of my child's life is in Your hands and I praise You for that. I ask that he (she) would look to You when his (her) life seems out of control, knowing that You are the author of the greatest lesson plan book of all. Let my baby rest in the peace that comes from relying on Your sovereignty. In Jesus' name I pray. Amen.

Day 7

Psalm 139:16 *All the days ordained for me were written in Your book, O Lord, before one of them came to be.*

Although we all may have planned for our death by purchasing life insurance and writing a will, overall, human beings frequently hope in a false immortality. I, for example, rarely go through my day believing it is my last. But as this psalm says, all of the days in our lives are set out for us before we are born. This means that we really cannot control how long we will be here and no matter how hard we try, we can't add an extra day to our lives. However, this also means that our lives will be no shorter than God plans for them to be. God will protect us until the day He has set for us expire. In the meantime, we must keep watch and be aware that at any moment the bridegroom, Christ, may return. We must prepare ourselves for that moment, just as much as the moment of death.

Lord, I thank You for Your great wisdom and for the plan You have created in my child's life. I rejoice in the fact that I can trust You to keep my baby safe until You call him (her) home. I pray that I will effectively teach my child to live a life that keeps You at the forefront of his (her) priorities. I ask that both he (she) and I would be watchful and ready as we live out our daily lives, for we know neither when You will return, nor when we will return to dust. In Jesus, name I pray. Amen.

Day 8

Proverbs 14:22 *Do not those who plot evil go astray? But those who plan what is good find love and faithfulness.*

No one wants to imagine his or her child plotting evil. However, we know that because they are human, our children have original sin. Although infants seem to possess the gift of innocence, this gift slowly fades as they remain in the world and are tainted by its sinfulness. As parents, we can teach our children the ways of the Lord and pray that they will follow Him, but ultimately the decision to follow Him will be their own. Let us take the time to plan for good in the lives of our children. We can do this through our own example and by praying that they will not stray from God's will but will follow Him faithfully.

Lord, I ask You to help me direct the life of my child. I want to teach him (her) Your ways so he (she) will depart from evilness. Please give my baby a strong desire to be obedient to You and let his (her) innocence last as long as possible. When the innocence of infancy fades and I see my child's unavoidable nature of original sin surface, I pray that he (she) would be repelled by it and would run to You to seek wisdom. Please enable me to teach my child to plan what is good for his (her) life so he (she) will find love and faithfulness in his (her) life. In Jesus' name I pray. Amen.

Day 9

Proverbs 16:3 *Commit to the Lord whatever You do and Your plans will succeed.*

I often find myself trying to control situations, especially those best left to God's control. Giving God full control of our lives is one of the greatest challenges that we face as humans. But if we do give God full control of our lives, is there any reason why we should make our own plans? This proverb answers that question for us. God does want us to make our own plans of our lives and He cares about the desires of our hearts. However, He wants us to commit our plans to Him. He wants us to seek Him for guidance through reading His word, praying and listening for the Holy Spirit's direction. For you see, our best plans are the ones that coincide with His will and it is only through spending time with Him that we can achieve this synchronization.

Lord, I ask You to speak to my heart so that its desires would reflect Your will. I pray that I would learn to commit all my plans, especially those for my child to You. You are Lord of my life and I want You to be Lord of his (hers) too. I ask that his (her) desires would reflect Your will as well and that he (she) would commit all he (she) does to You so that his (her) plans will succeed. Please call him (her) to Your ways and make him (her) a child after Your own heart. In Jesus' name I pray. Amen.

Day 10

Proverb 19:21 *Many are the plans in a man's heart but it is the Lord purpose that prevails.*

The plans we make in our daily lives can take many forms: a daily planner, a calendar of events, or even a list of yearly goals. These plans give our lives organization, focus and vision. When we make plans either for the weekend or for our next family vacation- we are sure to discover that our plans, as well thought out as they may be are only as effective as the plans that God has for us. All of the frustration that accompanies futile plans disappears when our plans are in synch with God's plan for our lives. Therefore, it is for the benefit of this harmony that we should pray for the plans of our hearts, seeking God's will in all that we determine to do.

Lord, I pray for the plans of my heart. I ask that the desires I have for my life will coincide with Your will for my life. I want to seek Your guidance in all that I aspire to do so that what I plan and what I am able to successfully accomplish with Your help will naturally coincide, both during my pregnancy and throughout my life. I also pray for the future plans of my child. I ask that he (she) would learn to seek Your will in his (her) life and that the Holy Spirit will give him (her) clear direction. Please speak to our hearts so that our desires and plans will coincide with Your purpose, which will always prevail. In Jesus' name I pray. Amen.

Day 11

Isaiah 14:24 *"Surely as I have planned so it will be and as I have purposed it so it will stand," says the Lord.*

God's plans and purposes stand firm against all opposition. Take, for example, the life of Moses. God's plan for his life was for him to lead his people out of captivity. Pharaoh had a different plan. He ordered that every Hebrew boy be thrown into the Nile river (Exodus 1:22). Whose plan stood? God's of course. Many Hebrew boys were killed, but Moses' mother put him in a basket and set him in the river, only to be found by the handmaids of Pharaoh's daughter. The princess raised him as the grandson of Pharaoh. Moses eventually rebelled against Pharaoh to answer the call of God. God's plans stand firm.

Lord, please bless the plans You have for my child. I praise You knowing that You stand firm in ensuring that Your purpose for his (her) life is the one that will prevail. Just as Moses' mother had faith in You when she set her son in the river, sparing his life, I pray for the same faith as a parent. Please keep it fresh in my mind that it is only Your plan for my child that will prevail in his (her) life. In times of worry and doubt, please let us rest in Your assurance and sovereignty. In Jesus' name I pray. Amen.

Day 12

Isaiah 14:27 *For the Lord Almighty has purposed and who can thwart Him? His hand is stretched out who can turn it back?*

Even though I know that no human is stronger than God, sometimes I feel as though the circumstances in my life here on earth could in some way overpower Him. But it is when I read a verse such as this one that I can experience the peace that the Holy Spirit has given me. The ways of God are the ways of life. There is neither a person nor a circumstance that can change God's plan. His hand will stand firmly stretched out over His children as he puts His plans for their lives into effect.

Lord, I pray today for Your peace. Please help me to experience this fruit of Your Holy Spirit as I contemplate the power of Your purpose. I know that You have determined a plan for my child's life. Therefore, there is no person and no circumstance that could change that plan. Nothing can remove the hand that You have outstretched over him (her). Please enable my child to rest in its protection, knowing that nothing will turn it back. In Jesus' name I pray. Amen.

Day 13

Isaiah 41:9 *"I took You from the ends of the earth, from its farthest corners I called you. I said, 'You are my servant'; I have chosen you and have not rejected you."*

There is no place on earth where one can hide from God, which can be seen as a good thing or a bad thing, depending on our point of view. When we sin we often try to hide from God as Adam and Eve did when they were disobedient. But just as they found no place in which they could hide from God, when we try to turn from Him, neither will we find a place to escape. God is the Creator of the earth. There is no where we can find where He will not be with us. This is not just a physical concept, but a personal one as well. No matter how much I try and shut down by ceasing from prayer, avoiding His Word or shunning church, God will not abandon me. The separation might have been my idea but as soon as I change my heart, He is right there with me. He has never left me; it is only me, thinking that I could be apart from Him. The sooner that I realize that there is no far corner to either the earth or my heart, where God does not exist, the sooner I can be the chosen one He desires to have as His servant.

Lord, please reach out to my child. Whenever he (she) has distanced himself (herself) please bring him (her) back to You. Show him (her) that the earth has no ends where You are void, nor does his (her) heart. Close any gaps that form in my child's heart. I do not want him (her) to be distanced from You at anytime. Please draw this baby to You like a magnet. Let him (her) feel Your acceptance as one of Your chosen people. Call my son (daughter) to You so he (she) can be the servant You desire and give him (her) the talents and will to serve You. In Jesus' name I pray. Amen.

Day 14

Isaiah 46:10 *"I make known the end from the beginning, from ancient times, what is still to come. I say: My purpose will stand and I will do all that I please.*

One of the best senses of accomplishment comes from starting and finishing a great task. And one of the greatest tasks in my life has been giving birth to my child. From the point of conception, through the nine months of growth and development to the moment of delivery, I oversaw the events of his prenatal life. This is how our entire lives are to God. He was there at the beginning of time and will be there at the end, already knowing what, when and where the end will be. I was blessed with seeing my baby's first breath and may or may not see his last, but I know that God oversees each breath, for He is the alpha and the omega.

Lord, You have created the earth and will bring it to its end. You alone know how the world began and how it will end. You also know the beginning and ending of my child's life. Your purpose for his (her) life will stand and I praise You for this. I also know that Your will is going to prevail in his (her) life and I pray that both he (she) and I will accept Your plan for our lives and use them to glorify You. In Jesus' name I pray. Amen.

Day 15

Isaiah 46:11 *"From the east I summon a bird of prey; from a far-off land a man to fulfill my purpose. What I have said, that I will bring about; what I have planned, that I will do."*

In one of the last scenes of *Lord of the Rings: Return of the King*, the protagonist Frodo and his friend are stranded on a rock surrounded by lava. They have, in essence, just saved the world and now seem to be at the brink of death, until from above two birds of prey fly in to rescue them. This event seems to best illustrate what the prophet Isaiah is saying to his people in Chapter 46, verse 11. If it is God's plan to rescue you, He will. He can summon birds of prey from the east and use men in far-off lands, even ungodly people, to fulfill His purpose. What He plans will come to be. No situation is out of His control.

Lord, I praise You for Your mighty power. You can use whatever means You want, both the obvious and the obscure to ensure that Your plans and purposes will come to be. I ask today that You would plan a fruitful and blessed life for my child. Please give him (her) the gift of faith so that he (she) will have peace and security in his (her) life, knowing that he (she) can rest in the endurance of Your plans and purposes. In Jesus' name I pray. Amen.

Day 16

Isaiah 49:1 *Before I was born the Lord called me; from my birth He made mention of my name.*

If we are ever to have any question about whether or not God is in control, the answer becomes evident in this verse. God calls us before we are born and makes mention of our name at the time of our birth. He is with us in the beginning of our lives and will be with us in the end. Although we cannot imagine our existence before our birth, God knows the exact details because He was there with us. When we are born, He calls our name. He sends us into the world for a specific purpose, which many times involves finding out exactly what that purpose is.

Lord, I know that You have a purpose both for my life and the life of my child. Please enable me to keep this in mind as I encounter the many stresses of daily life. Also, please help me to parent my child in a way that remembers that You have a specific purpose for my child. I ask that You would help me cultivate that purpose in his (her) life. I know that You have met my child even before I will and that You are in control of his (her) life and I thank You for that. In Jesus' name I pray. Amen.

Day 17

Isaiah 55:11 *"So is my word that goes out from my mouth: It will not return to me empty, but will accomplish what I desire and achieve the purpose for which I sent it.*

God's Word is an expression of His power. His Word has different forms. It is written in the Bible, it is spoken, either directly or through prophets and it is felt as the Holy Spirit. But no matter what form His Word takes, God declares that it will not return to Him empty. God completes all He sets out to accomplish and we can depend on Him to achieve the purpose of His will. God sends His Word to indicate the promises that He has for His children and ensures us that He will fulfill all that He has promised for our lives and the lives of our children.

Lord, please speak to my baby. Let him (her) be eager to seek Your Word. Give him (her) a love of reading Your Word through Bible stories or listening to me read them to him (her). Please give this child a strong desire to be filled with Your Spirit so that the line of communication between You and him (her) will be strong and formed early on in his (her) life. I praise You knowing that all You have purposed and desired for my child's life will be accomplished. In Jesus' name I pray. Amen.

Day 18

Jeremiah 1:5 *"Before I made you in your mother's womb, I chose you. Before you were born I set you apart for a special work. I appointed you as a prophet to the nations."*

In this verse, God is speaking to the prophet Jeremiah when he is just a boy. God tells him of the plans that he has made for his life. Through God's words to Jeremiah, the origin of our own lives should be made clear. It is God who chooses a child of His own and determines a plan for him (her). He places the child in your womb to grow and be born and live a life that glorifies Him. Not only does God have a specific plan for your child before he (she) grows in the womb, but your child has a specific role in God's broader plan for humanity as well. As your child lives out his (her) life in accordance with God's will, doing the special work He set out for him (her), he (she) will bring glory to God.

Lord, I thank You for forming this child in my womb and for choosing to give him (her) to me. I ask that You would set him (her) apart for special work. Please design a perfect plan for his (her) life so that through his (her) time here on earth he (she) can use his (her) time to glorify You. I know that his (her) life has a specific purpose in Your plan for humanity and I pray that You would give him (her) the courage and obedience to fulfill that role. In Jesus' name I pray. Amen.

Day 19

Jeremiah 10:23 *I know, O Lord, that a man's life is not his own; It is not for man to direct his steps.*

When this verse says that a man's life is not his own, it does not mean that we do not have free will. Of course we are the ones who make choices and decisions in our lives. However, the way we make the best decisions is by seeking God's wisdom in our lives. In Proverbs chapter 8 verses 10-11, Solomon writes of the importance of seeking God's direction for our lives. *"Choose my instruction instead of silver, knowledge rather than gold, for wisdom is more precious than rubies and nothing you desire compares with her."* Solomon is known for his wisdom and advises us here to seek God's will for our lives, knowing that our best steps will be those under His direction.

Lord, I pray that You would grant me wisdom. As a parent, I will have to make many decisions regarding my child and I ask that You would provide me with guidance from the Holy Spirit as to how I should act. I desire to parent my child in a way that is pleasing to You and I know this means taking each step under Your direction. I ask that You would also grant wisdom to my child. Let him (her) value wisdom above all earthly treasures so the he (she) will be blessed, for Your Word tell us, "Blessed is the man who finds wisdom, the man who gains understanding, for she is more profitable than silver and yields better returns than gold" *(Proverbs 3:13-14). In Jesus' name I pray. Amen.*

Day 20

Jeremiah 29:11 *"For I know the plans I have for you,"* *declares the Lord, "plans to prosper you and not harm you, plans to give you hope and a future."*

This verse continues to support the concept of God's sovereignty in our lives. He knows the plan He has for our children. He has designed a specific life for each of them. The lives God promises for our children are ones with prosperity and hope as well as a specific future. Dear parent, I know that each of us weave dreams for our children, but we must remember that it is God's will that must reign in our lives and the lives of our children.

Lord, I thank You for planning my child's life at the beginning of time. You know the plans You have for him (her) and I ask You to give me the courage to trust You, knowing that Your plan for my child includes prosperity. It may not always be evident to me or obvious in my eyes, but I ask that You will provide the hope and future for him (her) that You promise and that I would be able to support my child in a way that enables him (her) to live in the hope of this future. In Jesus' name I pray. Amen.

Day 21

Jeremiah 32:19 *Great are Your purposes and mighty are Your deeds.*

In this verse, the prophet Jeremiah proclaims that God's purposes are great and His deeds are mighty. He will do great things in our children's lives if we seek after them. God is more powerful than we can imagine and His power is ours for the asking. His Word tells us to seek and we will find, to ask and it will be given to us (Matthew 7:7). If we seek God's power we will be given mighty deeds to accomplish and if we teach our children to seek His power He will give them mighty deeds to perform as well.

Lord, I praise You for the greatness of Your purpose and for the mightiness of Your deeds. You are omnipotent. I ask that You would give my baby a life with great purpose. Please give him (her) the ability to clearly see the plans You have for his (her) life and to follow Your calling faithfully. Let this child clearly hear Your voice and give him (her) the courage to obey You when You call. I desire for him (her) to accomplish mighty deeds in Your name and for Your purpose. I ask this in Jesus' name. Amen.

Day 22

Matthew 18:14 *Jesus said, "Your Father in Heaven is not willing that any of these little ones should be lost.*

Jesus used the children in His ministry to illustrate His teachings. He especially highlights their innocence and their faith. In this verse, Jesus speaks of both the value that children have in God's eyes as well as God's will for His children. When Jesus says that it is not his Father's will that any of His children should be lost, He exhibits the Father's strong desire for all of His children to follow Him and seek Him. However, God knows that because He has given us free will not every child that is born will become a follower of Him. Therefore, we must do everything we can as parents to ensure that our child does not become a lost sheep, and the most important thing we can do is to lift our child up to God in prayer, petitioning for our child's salvation.

Lord, I bring my child before You and I ask that he (she) would be one of the sheep accounted for in Your flock. I do not desire for him (her) to depart from You or to go astray. I pray that I can be a parent that glorifies You through my example, my teaching and my prayers. Please give me the desire to constantly lift my child up to You in prayer so that he (she) will surely be secured in Your kingdom. If my child does stray from You during his (her) life, please give me the guidance to handle each situation as a godly mother and to rest patiently in Your timing, knowing that Your love for my child exceeds all of mine and that it is not Your will that he (she) should be lost. In Jesus' name I pray. Amen.

Day 23

Acts 17:26 *From one man, He made every nation of men, that they should inhabit the whole earth; and He determined the times set for them and the exact places where they should live.*

This verse declares God's sovereignty over our origins as well as our present day lives. Each of us has descended from one man. From Adam and Eve the whole earth has been populated from the beginning of time until today, giving our origins specificity. There is nothing random about our existence. God has not only determined our origins but has also delineated the times and places of our lives. He determines the era, the year, the country, the town, the family- every specific detail of our lives and our child's life. He has placed him (her) in your life with a specific plan in mind. God's plan involves your life as much as your child's life. For this baby is also a descendent of Adam and Eve and God has set an exact time and place for this baby, which is here and now.

Lord, I thank You for creating one man and one woman so that I could be a direct descendent of them and continue Your line of creation. I praise You for giving me the earth to inhabit and for Your sovereignty, which can be traced through time from beginning to end. I thank You Lord for giving me a place in Your history as well as for giving me this child in Your perfect timing and Your perfect placement. You have a specific plan for him (her) and I ask that I would be able to accept Your will in both his (her) life as well as in mine. In Jesus' name I pray. Amen.

Day 24

Romans 8:28 *And we know that in all things God works for the good of those who love Him, who have been called according to His purpose.*

This verse is reflective of the Old Testament story of King David and his wife Bathsheba. In an intriguing story of love and murder, King David has an affair with his friend's wife Bathsheba, who becomes pregnant while her husband is away at war. Trying to hide his adultery, David has her husband Uriah killed by sending orders the army leader to put him in the front lines while pulling back the troops. Once the prophet Nathan pointed out his sins to him, David was ashamed and repented. God spared David but took his son as punishment. Although David mourned the death of his son, he would eventually see how God transformed his sin into good. The next son born to David and Bathsheba was named Solomon. Solomon grew up to reign over Israel for many years, but is best known for his wisdom as expressed in his authorship of the books of Proverbs, Ecclesiastes, and Song of Songs. Even though David had sinned, God used his sin for good because God knew that David loved Him, as a man after His own heart.

Lord, You are a great transformer. Not only can You remove our sins from us, as far as the east is from the west, You can also use Your love to transform what is evil in our lives into goodness. God, I thank You for Your forgiveness and I ask that You would give my child a heart like David's. I know my child cannot be sinless, but I pray that when he (she) does sin, he (she) will be quick to repent. I pray that You would work goodness into all things in his (her) life. In Jesus' name I pray. Amen.

Day 25

Romans 8:29 *For those God foreknew He also predestined to be conformed to the likeness of His son, that He might be the firstborn among many brothers. And those He predestined, He also called.*

There are many first signs of pregnancy: nausea, fatigue, a missed period. These signs are the first indicators of the new life within you, leading you to believe that you are the first to know about this child. But long before you find yourself with two lines on a pregnancy test, God knows what the future nine months hold in store. He has known your baby from the beginning of time and has predestined his (her) life with you. Our children are created in the likeness of God's son. They are His brothers and sisters. Let us prepare our children well for such an honor.

Lord, I praise You for giving me Your Son to be firstborn as a sibling to both me and my child. I also thank You for creating this child in Your image. You have perfectly crafted him (her) and the image You have given him (her) is just starting to form as he (she) grows in my womb. I pray that my baby would continue to grow perfectly in Your image. And I also ask that I would be able to raise him (her) to be a worthy sibling to the brother You have given him (her) through Your Son, Christ Jesus. In Jesus' name I pray. Amen.

Day 26

2 Corinthians 5:5 *Now it is God who has made us for this very purpose and has given us the Spirit as a deposit guaranteeing what is to come.*

This verse testifies to the purposes that God has created for His children to fulfill. One of these purposes is for us to transform our mortality into eternal life. We are all born mortal, with a specific birth and death date. However, God does not intend for our lives to end at the time of our death. He has given us the gift of eternal life so that we can live with Him forever. This gift was made available through the death of His Son and is made true in our lives once we accept Jesus as our personal savior and confess our sins to Him. When Jesus ascended into heaven He left with us the gift of the Holy Spirit both so that we would not be alone and as a deposit guaranteeing the promise of eternal life.

Lord, I thank You for the many gifts You have given me, including the gift of Your Son. Through His death and resurrection, He guaranteed eternal life for everyone who accepts Him as his or her personal savior. I pray for this salvation for my child. I ask that he (she) would accept You as his (her) savior early in life. Please let the faith You give him (her) as a child continue throughout his (her) lifetime and let his (her) heart be filled with the Holy Spirit so that he (she) will truly be a child of God. In Jesus' name I pray. Amen.

Day 27

Ephesians 1:11 *In Him we were also chosen having been predestined according to the plan of Him who works out everything in conformity with the purpose of His will.*

God chooses each of us. He chooses to give us life and to call us to Him. This calling is not based on anything we do, but rather on the grace that has been provided for all of us through the death of His Son, Jesus Christ. He has predestined each of us to be a part of His sovereign plan. Everything that happens to us is a result of His will. Does this mean that God causes bad things to happen to us just as He does the good things? God does allow trials and difficulties in our lives. He does not promise that our lives will be easy. He does however promise that everything that happens in our lives will work out for good as it fulfills the purpose of His will. Just as we experience difficulty in our lives, our children will experience difficulties in their lives too, no matter how much we try to protect them. Although we may suffer more by just watching our children go through hardship than they will suffer actually going through it, when we view this as part of God's plan we can feel secure knowing God will use the negative to produce more positive than we could ever imagine.

Lord, I know that at some point my child will experience hardship and I ask for Your strength now so that we would be able to get through those times with Your help. Keep Your will foremost in my mind and help me show my child that You will use everything that happens in our lives for good through Your sovereign purpose. I thank You for choosing this child for me and for pre-determining his (her) life through Your will. I know that I can be secure in knowing that his (her) life is in Your hands. In Jesus' name I pray. Amen.

Day 28

Ephesians 2:10 *For we are God's workmanship, created in Christ to do good works, which God prepared in advance for us to do.*

Not only has God created our children in His image, but He has also created certain roles for them that He wants fulfilled throughout their lives. He gives each of His children specific talents and expects that they will use these talents to accomplish good works, which He has prepared in advance for them to do. One work that He has prepared for us, is that of being a mother. As mothers we have many challenges ahead of us. The greatest of these is the ability to raise our children in a way that develops a willing and able heart so that when God reveals the works He has prepared for them to do, they are ready and able to accomplish these works.

Lord, I thank You now for all the good works You have prepared in advance for my child. I ask that I would be able to provide opportunities for him (her) to develop his (her) talents. Please show my child early on in life what it is You have chosen as his (her) talent. Please give him (her) the desire and the means to develop these gifts. I also ask that You would help me foster a desire in him (her) to complete these works and that he (she) would be willing to serve You throughout his (her) life. Please provide him (her) with many opportunities for service and let him (her) be a member of a strong church body so that he (she) would have numerous occasions to be a servant of God. In Jesus' name I pray. Amen.

Day 29

Philippians 2:13 *For it is God who works in You to will and to act according to His purpose.*

God works in us through the Holy Spirit. Because of the presence of the Holy Spirit, we are able to do the will of God. However, the Holy Spirit is constantly being opposed by temptation in our lives. Satan tempts us not only to resist the guidance of the Holy Spirit, but also to ignore its presence altogether. Because of this constant battle, it is imperative that we put on the armor of God so we can be successful in the battle of spiritual warfare. For in Ephesians 6:11 we are told to, "*Put on the full armor of God so that you can take your stand against the devil's schemes.*" If God is to work in us through the Holy Spirit we must be ready to battle opposition.

Lord, I praise You for the gift of the Holy Spirit and I ask that You would enable my child to feel His presence strongly, hear His guidance and be obedient in his (her) actions. I know that he (she) will face spiritual warfare and I pray that more often than not, he (she) will win over the temptation. I ask that You would show this child how to use Your weapons to defeat the power of Satan as he tries to draw him (her) from You. Please hold my child tightly in Your hand so You can work through him (her) in fulfilling Your will and acting according to Your purposes. In Jesus' name I pray. Amen.

Day 30

2 Timothy 1:9 *[God] has saved us and called us to a holy life-not because of anything we have done, but because of His own purpose and grace.*

Every action has an equal and opposite reaction. I learned Newton's Third Law of Motion in a twelfth grade physics class. Although it is a law of motion, it is also reflective of the world we live in. We believe that we can earn a successful life by working hard, doing what is right and generally being a "good person." I have seen this concept work to some extent many times in our society. However this law of motion applies in no way to our relationship with God. Although He does desire for us to work hard in developing our relationship with Him, there is nothing we can "do" to earn God's grace. God's grace is a gift from Him to us. We cannot produce it by working hard or doing good deeds. His grace comes to us solely through the death and resurrection of Jesus Christ. This is not to say that hard work and kindness are futile, they just won't enable you to earn salvation. In God's eyes we are all sinners, but He has made salvation available to both us and our children through the living sacrifice of His Son.

Lord, I thank You for the gift of salvation that You have made available through Jesus' death and resurrection. I am redeemed in Your eyes. I thank You that You have made Your grace a gift and that I don't have to work to earn it, but that I can receive it through Jesus' sacrifice. I pray right now to renew the acceptance of Jesus as my savior in my heart and I ask that You would call my child to Your great purpose as well. Please open his (her) eyes to the gift of Your grace and lead his (her) heart to seek You as his (her) savior. In Jesus' name I pray. Amen.

Month 5:
The Promise of Love

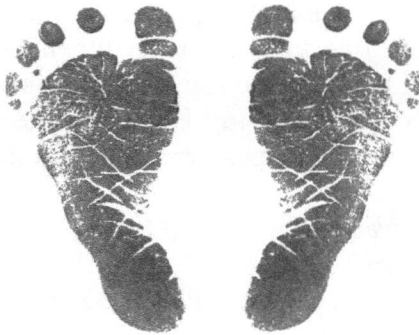

Day 1

Exodus 34:6 *And He passed in front of Moses, proclaiming, the Lord, the Lord, the compassionate and gracious God, slow to anger, abounding in love and faithfulness, maintaining love to thousands.*

This is one of the few times where God has made Himself visible to mankind. When Moses went to the top of Mount Sinai to receive the Ten Commandments, God revealed Himself to Moses and used these words to describe Himself. One of the ways He portrays Himself is with the words "abounding love." God is love. As love, He is the opposite of fear. When we abide in His love, we are free from all fear. When God describes His love as being maintained to thousands, we can see that His love is limitless. He loves everything He has created, every creature that has lived on earth in the past, present and future.

Lord, I thank You for love. It is only Your love that drives out fear. Please make Your presence and Your love known to me as I continue in this pregnancy. Please keep all thoughts of fear from my mind. When my mind starts to wander, thinking harmful thoughts, I pray that I will turn off the fearful flow and will seek You. Lord, You are compassionate, gracious and abounding in love. You have shown Your love to all of creation. Please enable me to abide in it now so that all the fears I have with this pregnancy will vanish. In Jesus' name I pray. Amen.

Day 2

Psalm 6:4 *Turn O Lord and deliver me; save me because of Your unfailing love.*

God is the Great Deliverer. He has delivered His people from infinite hardships throughout time. We can turn to the examples of Old Testament figures such as Moses and David to see how God used His unfailing love to deliver His people from adversity. He delivered the Israelites from being Egyptian slaves under the leadership of Moses. He kept David from being killed by his enemies. These men sought God for deliverance and He answered their prayers. Although they faced trying circumstances, they had nothing to fear because they knew that God's will was for them to prevail. They were saved because of His everlasting love for them and it is this same kind of love that can save us from any circumstances that we may face.

Lord, Your love is unfailing. It will not fail against the most difficult of earthly circumstances. Whether my circumstances are enslaving or even deadly, I know that it is Your will and Your love that will never fail. Lord, as I prepare to deliver this baby I know that I may face difficult circumstances and great pain. It will only be the strength and unfailing love that You provide that will keep me from defeat. Lord, please deliver me from delivery! Keep me and my baby safe. Please let the pain be minimal and let me endure it with Your great power. In Jesus' name I pray. Amen.

Day 3

Psalm 13:15 *But I trust in Your unfailing love; my heart rejoices in Your salvation. I will sing to the Lord, for He has been good to me.*

Trusting in God's love enables us to escape fear. Whatever brings fear into our lives can be disengaged by the power of God's love. When we seek God's love in our lives we can rejoice in the salvation that comes from God. It is only God who can save us from the desperate circumstances of life. We can seek His love through prayer, meditation and the message that is made available in God's Word. Through God's love we can find ourselves free from fear. Death is one of fear's strongest agents. Throughout time the fear of death has had an impermeable grip over man's heart. However, God has provided us with a means to be saved from the shadow of death. For the believer, who has accepted Christ into his heart and repented of his sins, God offers salvation through everlasting life. He has promised us a place in his heavenly kingdom where fear has no existence.

Lord, I thank You for the salvation that You have offered us through the sacrifice of Your son. Through His death and resurrection we are able to escape the fear of death. You have the power to set me free not only from death, but from all fear that may arise from the circumstances in my life. Please set me free from all fears today. Keep me from being a slave to fear and grant me the peace that comes from abiding in Your love. Lord, I sing Your praises today, knowing that through Your love and all that it promises, You will be good to me. In Jesus' name I pray. Amen.

Day 4

Psalm 18:5-7 *In my anguish I cried to the Lord, and he answered me by setting me free. The Lord is with me, I will not be afraid...The Lord is with me; He is my helper.*

It is only God who can set us free from fear for it is Him who can ensure us love. He keeps us from the anguish that fear can cause in our lives if we live under its control. If we realize that God is with us constantly, there is nothing that should scare us for His love is omnipotent. When we rest in His presence, praying and seeking His Word, it will become evident that His love chases away all fear. He is our helper. He will help us through any circumstance we face. All we have to do is ask and believe.

Lord, I thank You for Your love. You have answered so many of my prayers and I praise You for that. Just knowing that I am in Your presence keeps me from being afraid. I ask that You would always be with me so that I can be free from fear. Lord, please be with me especially during this time. For it is now, with my child's life and first breath before me that the many problems that could arise creep into my mind, attempting to make me crippled by the fear they invoke. Lord, I ask You to be my helper. Please relieve me from any anguish my situation may bring and keep Your love in the forefront of my mind. In Jesus' name I pray. Amen.

Day 5

Psalm 27:1 *The Lord is my light and my salvation. Whom shall I fear? The Lord is the stronghold of my life- of whom shall I be afraid?*

Most scary movies are filmed with the least amount of light possible because directors know that it is darkness that invokes fear. However, it is not so much the absence of light that makes us fearful, but rather the presence of the unknown. When darkness prevails in our lives, it hides what the light makes familiar. Darkness creates the unknown and it is the unknown that makes us tremble. Nevertheless, we do not have to rely on our eyes for light in our lives, for God is the strongest light available to us. He dismisses darkness and brings forth truth. He makes known all that is hidden by darkness and in doing so removes fear. When God is our light and the stronghold of our lives, fear is powerless.

Lord, I want you to be the light in my life. Please remove all darkness from my mind. Whenever the darkness of the unknown begins to cloud my life, please erase all fear. Lord, be the stronghold in my life so there is nothing that will bring me fear. As I face the darkness of the unknown, I ask that Your presence would shine so brightly that I would feel only Your love as I face the future and the amazing changes that the next few weeks will bring into my life. In Jesus' name I pray. Amen.

Day 6

Psalm 33:13-15 *From heaven the Lord looks down and sees all mankind. From His dwelling place, He watches all who live on earth- He who formed the hearts of all, who considers everything they do.*

I have written before of God's omnipresence and how when we abide in His presence we will experience His love in place of any of our fears. In this verse, God is described as looking down on us from heaven, which is probably how most of us think of God, sitting up there looking down on all we do. But God is never distanced from us. He is as close to us as our next prayer and has given us the gift of the Holy Spirit to live within our hearts, so we can feel God's presence at all times. He has formed each of us and as His creation, He has great love for us.

Lord, I know that You are in heaven looking down on me unceasingly. You are watching every aspect of my life, like a play before Your eyes, where You are the director. You have created me and You consider everything I do. Please consider me now Lord. Watch over me closely during this time in my life. I know only You can see the future and I pray that as You watch over me and my child as he (she) comes to life, our futures would be secure in Your love for us. In Jesus' name I pray. Amen.

Day 7

Psalm 34:4 *I sought the Lord and he answered me and delivered me from all my fears.*

In this psalm David is praising God for answered prayer. In the previous psalms, we see that David's desperate circumstances led him to call on God for freedom from his plight as much as his fear. When we seek God for freedom from fear, we can rest in His love, knowing that we will be able to share in praises of answered prayer and deliverance. God is love. God loves all He has created and will grant the peace that comes from abiding in His love to all who seek freedom from fear.

Lord, I praise You for Your love. You dissipate all fear through Your embodiment of love. When I seek Your love, You make Your presence known and when I am afraid You deliver me from my fears. You alone are God, the terminator of human fear and the bearer of light and love. Please answer my prayer today Lord as You answered the prayers of David so many years ago. Keep my mind from being crippled by fear of the unknown. Please enable me to rest in the love that comes from no other source. Deliver me from all my fears and help me to seek Your love at all times. In Jesus' name I pray. Amen.

Day 8

Psalm 46:1 *God is our refuge and strength, an ever-present help in trouble. Therefore we will not fear.*

Pregnancy doesn't necessarily have to be a time of trouble, but it definitely is a time of change. You will experience physical and emotional changes as you grow a child within you. Change can be fearful because it involves the unknown and it can also bring on trouble because it requires that adjustments be made. If you do experience trouble through your pregnancy and delivery, God's Word ensures that He will be your refuge and your strength. The promise of God's protection enables us to be free from fear. He is an ever-present help. Whenever assistance is needed, all that needs to be done is cry out to Him in prayer and He will alleviate any trouble that this pregnancy may bring about.

Lord, I praise You for Your qualities of protection. You are the perfect source of refuge and strength. I look to You during this pregnancy for refuge from any fears or troubles that I may encounter as I bring this baby into the world. Please strengthen both my mind and my body as I grow this child within me. Protect me from negative thoughts that may be caused by hormones. I look to You Lord, knowing that You are an ever-present help. Your presence in my life will keep me from being afraid I as experience each of the changes that accompany this pregnancy. In Jesus' name I pray. Amen.

Day 9

Psalm 56:3 *When I am afraid, I will trust in You. In God, whose word I praise, in God I trust, I will not be afraid.*

We know that love can keep us from fear. If we can trust in God's love for us we can be free of fear. When we are afraid, we are showing God that we do not trust Him to provide for us and that we do not believe that He knows what is best for us. Even if our lives are full of pain and suffering, if we are living out God's plan for our lives, then we are living out God's will and there is nothing that we could get out of life that will bring us more joy. If we trust in God we do not have to be afraid for we will know that every event of this life is under His jurisdiction and part of His sovereign plan.

Lord, I love You and I praise You for Your love for me. Because I know that You love me, I do not have to be afraid. Lord, I pray that You would keep me from pain and suffering, especially during this pregnancy. I pray that I would trust in You instead of running fearful thoughts through my mind. Lord, please help me trust You during this pregnancy. Resting in the sovereignty of Your will ensures my protection from fear. I pray for that protection in my life. In Jesus' name I pray. Amen.

Day 10

Psalm 91:1-4 *He who dwells in the shelter of the Most High will rest in the shadow of the Almighty. I will say of the Lord, "He is my refuge and my fortress, my God in whom I trust." Surely He will save you from the fowler's snare and from the deadly pestilence. He will cover you with his feathers, and under His wings you will find refuge; His faithfulness will be your shield and rampart.*

The words of this psalm became familiar to me as I sung the hymn "On Eagle's Wings" in church each Sunday. However, I never really knew what the word "fowler" meant. Looking it up in a Bible dictionary, I found that in Biblical times many men took jobs as fowlers, or bird hunters. So, using this illustration, God is telling us that He will save us from any traps in which we may find ourselves. Notice that He is not saying we will never be trapped, or experience pain, but that when we are ensnared we can turn to God to rescue us. Continuing the bird illustration, God tells us that He will protect us with His feathers and wings. As God likens himself to a bird, we can associate Him with the image of a hen caring for her baby chicks. Like an instinctive fowl, God will protect us with His love.

Lord, I praise You for Your love. I know that during my life I will face areas of entrapment and pestilence. But as I live through difficult times, I know that You will provide me with safety and refuge. Lord, please keep both me and my baby safe during this pregnancy. As my baby grows in my womb and exists during delivery, I pray that we will feel Your protection. Just as mother birds instinctively care for their young in nature, I know that You will protect us, Your children. Also, I ask that You would please help me to be the kind of parent who brings You glory, who guides and protects her children from the dangers of the world. In Jesus name I pray. Amen.

Day 11

Psalm 100:5 *For the Lord is good and His love endures forever; His faithfulness continues through all generations.*

God is good. He embodies everything that goodness is. We can aspire to reach a godly level of goodness, but we will always be sinners. No matter how many times or to what degree we sin, God will forever offer His love to us as we repent. God is also faithful. He has kept His covenants from the beginning of time. His promises are still true today and will continue until He comes again. This means that whatever God has promised us, will also be true for our children, grandchildren, and all of our ancestors. The promise will be there, as will the choice. It is up to us to teach our children the ways and promises of God and then to pray that they will accept Him as their savior, repenting from their sins and welcoming His Son Jesus Christ into their lives. And it is up to them to decide to follow Christ. This acceptance will enable our children to experience God's goodness, love and faithfulness in their lives as they become children of God.

Lord, You are good. The model You have given us in Your Son shows us exactly how You want us to live. Please help me to be good and when I am not, I ask that I would quickly become aware of my sin and repent. Lord, I pray that I would abide not only in Your goodness, but also in Your love and the faithfulness of Your promises as I bring this child into the world. Lord, I also want my baby to know Your goodness, Your love and Your faithfulness. Please help him (her) come to accept You as his (her) Savior. I pray that Your Holy Spirit would convict my child of his (her) sins and make his (her) heart open for repentance. In Jesus' name I pray. Amen.

Day 12

Psalm 145:13 *The Lord is faithful to all his promises and loving toward all He has made.*

God will keep His promises and will love us, for we are part of His creation. God has promised to love us and has made His love most evident in the gift of His Son. We often give gifts to those we love, but there is no better gift in existence than the gift of eternal life. God has promised His people a means of redemption and through the loving gift of His Son, we have been granted salvation from death. Because of God's promise and love for us, we will be with Him in heaven for eternity.

Lord, I thank You for Your promises and Your love. You are faithful in all You pledge to accomplish and loving to all Your children. I lay claim to these promises for my baby and myself today. Please keep Your promises for our lives and show us Your unending love. I ask that as my baby grows in this world, he (she) would be aware of the promises You have made to him (her) as one of Your children. Please let this baby be aware of Your love for him (her) as early as possible in his (her) life because feeling Your love and abiding in it will help him (her) to be protected from fear. In Jesus' name I pray. Amen.

Day 13

Isaiah 35:4 *Say to those with fearful hearts, "Be strong and do not fear; your God will come."*

God is the Great Consoler. Through the prophet Isaiah, God tells his people that He will come and because of His presence, His people should have no reason to fear. Just as we console our children from the fear of a bad dream or of the darkness of their bedrooms at night, trying to relieve their fears with our love and our presence, God consoles His children as well. God wants His children to be free from fear. He does not desire for us to be afraid, but rather for us to find comfort in His love and presence. He asks for us to be strong, promising that He will come into our lives. When we accept Jesus Christ as our Savior, we are welcoming God's Spirit into our hearts. And, as we make room for God in our hearts, there is less room for fear in our minds. God has given us the gift of the Holy Spirit so we can have God's love living in us and helping us to drown out any fearful thoughts.

Lord, I praise You for Your loving presence. Thank You for sending Your Son and giving us Your Holy Spirit to live within us. It is Your presence in my life that enables me to abide in Your love and conquer any fears I may face. Just as my child comes to me for comfort from his (her) fears, I seek Your consolation from my own fears of labor and delivery and again I ask You to come into my life and use Your love to drive out all fear from my mind. In Jesus' name I pray. Amen.

Day 14

Isaiah 38:17b *In all Your love, You kept me from the pit of destruction.*

God's love protects us. In this verse, He has saved King Hezekiah from the pit of destruction. Even though we may not find ourselves trapped in a giant hole in the ground, each of us may encounter such a "pit" in our lives. As you go into labor, you may fear the "pits" of pain, injury or even death. Although there is a chance that you may encounter these "pits," God's love for you will deliver you from destruction. He does not promise that you will be free from these tribulations, but He does promise that His love will keep you from being paralyzed by fear of them. Let's face it, you will experience labor pains but God's love will keep you from total destruction, for even death will not overpower the eternal life we have promised to us through Christ.

Lord, I praise You for Your gift of love and I ask that Your love would keep me from the "pits" of destruction in my life. Lord, please help me as I go through the pain of labor and protect me from injury and death. Please keep my baby safe during this time as well. If we do have to face any tragedies, I pray that we can do it with Your love, knowing that whatever trials we face, Your love will keep us from destruction. In Jesus' name I pray. Amen.

Day 15

Isaiah 41:10 *"So do not fear, for I am with you; do not be dismayed for I am your God. I will strengthen you and help you; I will uphold you with my righteous hand."*

In this verse, God tells us that we have no reason to fear because He is with us. God is love and so when we are aware of His presence, we are also most aware of His love. God's love for us keeps us from being dismayed. He promises to give us His strength and His help, a promise we can most assuredly use during our pregnancy. When we seek God's strength and His help, we have an almighty power to which no fear can survive. God also promises to uphold us with his righteous hand. There is no better support on which to lean as you journey through pregnancy.

Lord, as I face the numerous fears of pregnancy, I ask that You would be with me. Please fill me with Your love so I can face each day with a fearless mind. Lord, uphold me with Your righteous hand and let me lean on Your strength in my weakest moments. I turn to You as I face adversity and fear so that I will not be dismayed, but will find solace in Your loving presence. In Jesus' name I pray. Amen.

Day 16

Isaiah 41:13 *"For I am the Lord your God who takes hold of your right hand and says to you do not fear, I will help you."*

There are some moments in life when there is nothing we want more than someone to hold our hand. Being in labor is one of those times. Although there are few things that will comfort you during this painful time, someone grabbing your hand in love will bring you a bit of solace. I was blessed to have my husband with me during labor, but I sympathize with women whose circumstances lead them to give birth without a hand to hold. However, as God promises in this verse, He will take hold of your right hand and tell you not to fear. He will help you through this difficult time because His love for you is so great. Even if you are physically alone, God's presence is always with you, showing you love and keeping you from harm.

Lord, I praise You for Your love. I pray that You would keep me safe through my pregnancy and labor. Please let me feel Your grip as You take hold of my right hand and help me through the difficulties of this time. Lord, fill me with Your spirit so that by abiding in Your presence I will be kept from fear. I ask that if I do become fearful I would quickly remember that Your righteous hand is reaching out to me at all times, upholding me and keeping me safe. In Jesus' name I pray. Amen.

Day 17

Isaiah 43:2 *"When you pass through the waters, I will be with you and when you pass through the rivers they will not sweep over you, when you walk through the fire you will not be burned; the flames will not set you ablaze."*

Almost daily the evening news features a story on a natural disaster somewhere in the world. Floods, hurricanes and wildfires seem to make the best news stories, probably because they invoke fear as people realize their lack of power against nature. Weather is something to which humans have conceded control. We can make provisions and try to protect ourselves, but ultimately we are at the mercy of the elements. It is only God who can protect us and He promises to do so in this verse. God does not promise to keep us sheltered from all of life's storms, but he does intend to keep us safe as we weather them. One of the stormiest times in your life can be your pregnancy and delivery. You may find yourself amid emotional and physical tempests. But from the time your water breaks through the fiery pains of labor, God promises to be with you and to keep you from being swept away or set ablaze.

Lord, I thank You for the protection Your love gives me in fearful times, such as this one. I know that this pregnancy and delivery may be hard on my body. I do not seek to avoid this pain, but rather to endure it with Your help. Please keep me from being consumed by the trials of pregnancy. Protect me from its storminess and let me abide securely in Your love. In Jesus' name I pray. Amen.

Day 18

Isaiah 43:4 *"You are precious and honored in my sight, I love you," says the Lord.*

We are all God's creations and because of the love that He has for us, we become precious and honored beings. God's gift of love is given to us based solely on His grace, not on our actions. We cannot earn God's love by "being good." For, try as we may to obey God, we are all sinners. We are imperfect alone but are made perfect through Christ's sacrifice. It is only through the cross that we have been made precious and honorable in God's eyes. Because of His love, God has given us His Son so we may share in His glory. As you give birth to your own child, pray for God's gift of grace for him (her) so he (she) may be precious and honored in His sight as well.

Lord, I thank You for Your love. You love me even though You know my sins, for it was You who created me. I also thank You for the gift of salvation that You have given me through the sacrifice of Your son Jesus Christ. I pray that as my child comes to life, he (she) will gladly accept Jesus as his (her) Savior as well. My baby will always be precious and honorable in my eyes, I pray that he (she) will come to You through Jesus so that You would share the same opinion of him (her). In Jesus' name I pray. Amen.

Day 19

Isaiah 43:5 "*Do not be afraid for I am with you; I will bring your children from the east and gather you from the west...everyone who is called by my name, whom I created for my glory, whom I formed and made.*"

God has given life to each of us and His love for us can protect us from anything that may cause us fear. He promises to bring our children from the east and to gather us from the west, which clarifies His jurisdiction over the earth. There is no place where we are out of God's reach. We are never too far from the grip of His righteous hand, neither physically nor spiritually. God will bring us together with the children he has planned for us to care for, whether through the process of giving birth or by alternate means. We share God as our creator, shaper and maker, and we are united in His love and His promise to be gathered together.

Lord, I praise You for the span of Your love, which reaches from the east to the west and I ask that I would never feel so far from You that I would believe that You could not reach me. Lord, as I prepare to meet my child, I pray that You would gather us together in Your perfect timing and under the protection of Your love. You have said that You will bring our children from the east and I pray that as You bring my child from my womb, You will keep him (her) safe and healthy through the journey, as Your child and under Your loving care. In Jesus' name I pray. Amen.

Day 20

Isaiah 44:1-2 *This is what the Lord says, He who made you and formed you in the womb and who will help you, "Do not be afraid."*

There are many things to be afraid of during pregnancy and labor, including the most haunting question, "What if something goes wrong?" But in these verses, God tells us that He has formed us in the womb, just as He has formed your child. If we are formed by God, we are not only created in His image, but are molded just as He has willed us to be. No matter how we judge perfection, each child is created to perfectly fulfill the will of God. God promises that He is the one who has flawlessly created your child and He is the one who will help you and because of this, you shall not be afraid.

Lord, please bless my child as You form him (her) in the womb. Please let him (her) grow into a person that will perfectly fulfill Your will for his (her) life. And as I bring this child to the point of living and breathing, please be my Helper. In fact, let me be the one who takes a back seat to You. Let me be a vessel of Your will, like clay in the hands of a potter. I lay claim to Your promise to help me today and I ask that by relying on Your help and Your sovereignty, I may free my mind from all fear. In Jesus' name I pray. Amen.

Day 21

Isaiah 54:10 *Though the mountains be shaken and the hills be removed, yet my unfailing love for you will not be shaken.*

I have never climbed a mountain. The largest mountain I've ever even seen has been part of the ski resorts of the Pocono mountain range in Pennsylvania. And I'm sure that as far as mountains go, I have been missing out. However, when I think of mountains, I still think of the same symbol of might that they are meant to represent in this verse. If we think about what it would take to shake a mountain we would, of course, be in awe of its power and would immediately be aware of the strength of God. But in this verse, we see that God's love is even more powerful than the power that could shake a mountain. If love that powerful reigns in our lives, how can there be any room for fear?

Lord, I praise You for the strength of Your unfailing love. I know that Your love is stronger than the power that can move the largest mountain on earth. Please help me to abide in Your love and keep Your presence in my mind so that fear would have no space to reign. Keeping fear from my mind may seem as hard as shaking a mountain, but with Your power and love I know that I can be free from all fear. Please give me that freedom today. In Jesus' name I pray. Amen.

Day 22

Jeremiah 3:31 *"I have loved you with an everlasting love, I have drawn you with loving kindness," says the Lord.*

We never have to fear losing God's love, for His love is everlasting. This means that it has the strength to endure in two directions, both across time and through difficulty. God has loved us from the beginning of our lives and will continue to love us unceasingly through our deaths and into our resurrected lives with Him in heaven. His love does not run out nor does it weaken in proportion to our sins. We may reject His love and rebel from His commands, but His love for us endures. He will continue loving us whether or not we reciprocate it. Therefore, we can resist all fear of losing His love, it will never retreat.

Lord, I thank You for the love that You have freely given to me. When You drew me into existence, Your love filled my being. I know that You will continue to love me throughout my life and I just ask that I will continue to be grateful for this gift. Lord, let me abide in Your love so that I can be free from fear. And as You are now drawing my child into existence, I ask that You would fill him (her) with Your everlasting love as well. Let this baby feel Your presence and Your kindness so he (she) will not be a slave to the fears of this world. In Jesus' name I pray. Amen.

Day 23

Jeremiah 17:7-8 *But blessed is the man who trusts in the Lord, whose confidence is in Him. He will be like a tree planted by the water that sends out its roots by the stream. It does not fear when the heat comes; its leaves are always green. It has no worries in a year of drought and never fails to bear fruit.*

When we trust in God's love we can find freedom from fear. Our confidence in God's sovereignty will keep us from being destroyed by fear. Like a tree planted by the water, your faith in God's love will keep you strong as you continue through this pregnancy. When the heat and pain of labor comes, you will not fear. Nor shall you worry through the delivery, knowing that with God's love, you will never fail to bear the fruit of His will.

Lord, I pray that I will be like a tree planted by the water. I want to send my roots by the stream, drawing from Your reservoir of love. Lord, please help me trust in You and put my confidence in You so I will not be afraid when I am faced with the heat of labor and the drought of contractions. Please keep the leaves of my heart green with Your love so I will be free from worries. And Lord, help me most of all to bear the fruit of this child with Your power and strength. In Jesus' name I pray. Amen.

Day 24

Zephaniah 3:17 *The Lord your God will take great delight in you. He will quiet you with His love, He will rejoice over you with singing.*

Upon first glance of the child you have given birth to you may feel an overwhelming sense of delight and joy. Just as we love our children and delight in them, God has the same feelings towards us as His children. He delights in us, rejoices over us and loves us. So many times I feel as though I disappoint God through my weakness, but this verse brings me comfort, knowing that God's love is not a love of obligation, but one of pleasure. The pleasure that my child brings me reflects the way that God feels about all of His children. As a new parent, you may also find yourself attempting to quiet your newborn with your love, through feeding, rocking or singing. Whatever the cause, your love for your child will bring you to try whatever you can to soothe him (her). Similarly, God desires to quiet our fears through the love that He provides for all of His children.

Lord, thank You for delighting in me. I ask that I would be the kind of servant that would continue to bring You pleasure. I ask that You would also delight in my child and rejoice over him (her) in singing. I also pray that I would be able to quiet my baby with my loving actions. I want to be the type of mother that delights in caring for her child and soothing him (her). I ask that You would also quiet the fears of my heart. As I begin to doubt Your power and control I ask that I would be able to hear Your voice as You rejoice over me with singing, knowing that Your love will keep me safe. In Jesus' name I pray. Amen.

Day 25

Romans 8:15 *For you did not receive a Spirit that makes you a slave to fear, but you received a Spirit of sonship. And by Him we cry Abba, Father. The Spirit Himself testifies with our Spirit, that we are God's children.*

The sacrifice that Jesus made for us on the cross enables us to receive the gift of eternal life through our repentance of sins and acceptance of Him as our savior. It also gave us the gift of sonship. We were made to be Christ's brothers and sisters and therefore children of God. Through His death and resurrection, we were given the gift of the Holy Spirit, a Spirit that has the power to drive our fear and to receive love.

Lord, I thank You for the gift of Your Son. Through His sacrifice He has granted me eternal life as well as a Spirit that drives out fear. Please drive out all the fear that this pregnancy may bring. Let me abide in Your love so I will not be a slave to fear. I cry out to You, Abba, Father, in this stressful time, asking for the Holy Spirit to fill me with Your love. In Jesus' name I pray. Amen.

Day 26

Hebrews 13:6 *The Lord is my helper I will not be afraid.*

When you face the task of delivering a child, you will need help. This help may come from doctors, nurses, spouses, or even medication, which can all play a vital part in your labor. However, the most effective helper that you can have during this time is the Lord Almighty. God can give us whatever we may need during the trial of our pregnancy, labor and delivery. This help may take the form of strength, safety, protection, love and peace. We know that God loves us and has our best interest in mind at all times, even though what we consider to be best may not match God's plan for us. However, trusting in His love and sovereignty will ensure that He can provide us with the effectiveness of His help.

Lord, I ask that You would bless all of those who have a role in my pregnancy and delivery. Please give wisdom and guidance to the doctors and nurses who will be taking part in my baby's birth. I also ask that You would be with my spouse during this time. Please keep him strong and supportive as he stands by me, for even though he may not be in pain, he may be flooded with emotions and exhaustion. Lord, if I am to take any medication, I ask that it would provide me relief and that I would be free from any side effects. Lord, I also ask for Your help. Please be with me during this time as my best helper. In Jesus' name I pray. Amen.

Day 27

2 Timothy 1:7 *For God did not give us a spirit of timidity, but a spirit of power, of love and of self-discipline.*

God gives us a spirit of power, love and self-discipline. He desires for us to use these gifts to defeat fear. When we pray for God's power and abide in His love, we can escape the anguish that fear can beset upon our minds. God's love is a gift for us and is made available through prayer. However, the disciplining of our mind is a responsibility left to us. Fear has only one stage on which to perform and that is in our mind. Through the control of self-discipline we can prevent fear from having power in our lives. Pregnancy can set the stage for fear because so much of what is happening to your body is new to you and at the same time is out of your control. As you face your fears you can seek God's love through prayer and take every thought captive, giving it no time to perform in your mind.

Lord, I praise You for giving me a Spirit of power, love and self-discipline. As my pregnancy continues, please give me the continued self-discipline to take every fearful thought captive, preventing it from taking root in my mind and making me its slave. Please enable me to abide in Your love so fear will have no power over me. In Jesus' name I pray. Amen.

Day 28

1 John 3:1 *How great is the love the Father has lavished on us, that we should be called children of God.*

The relationship that we have with our own children mirrors the one that God has with us. I believe that He enables us to be parents so that we can experience some of the same emotions that He does, especially the love that a parent has for his (her) child. As we grow as parents, we can equate our experiences and relationships with our own children as we also develop as children of God. We are God's children. He calls us His own. His love is a gift to us and we can better understand His love for us as we share love with the children He has given us.

Lord, I thank You for the love You have given me. I am honored to be called a child of God. I praise You for giving me the gift of a child so I can experience what it feels like to be a parent and to love with a parent's love. I feel blessed not only to be Your child, but also to be a parent to the child You have given me. I pray that I would parent him (her) in a way that would honor You. In Jesus' name I pray. Amen.

Day 29

1 John 4:16b-4:17 *God is love.* *Whoever lives in love, lives in God and God in him.* *In this way, love is made complete.*

God is love. This is a very powerful sentence. It defines who God is by illuminating his basic composition. Everything that the emotion of love encompasses is made available through the presence of God. When God lives in us, we can experience His love for ourselves and share it with others. God's presence in us gives us the ability to love other people, especially those who are "unlovely". His loving presence also gives us the power to drown out any fearful thoughts that may enter our minds. Fear can only be conquered by love. When we live in love, we live in God and He, therefore, lives in us. Residing with God enables us to be free from all fear.

Lord, I praise You, for You are love. I thank You for sharing that love with me. I ask that You would enable me to live in Your love. Let me feel Your love and help me share that love with others. Point out for me anyone that I may have trouble loving and show me how to love him (her) as You would. Lord, show me how to live in You so You can live in me. I want Your love to live in me so that I can be free from the grip of fear. Please teach me to rest in Your love. In Jesus' name I pray. Amen.

Day 30

1 John 4:18 *There is no fear in love but perfect love drives out fear because fear has to do with punishment. The one who fears is not made perfect in love.*

For me, the most frightening part of pregnancy was labor. I was afraid both of the pain and the unknown. However, these emotions of fear are ungodly, for God is not a God of fear, but a God of love. Driving fear out of your mind is no easy task. The most effective way to conquer fear is through prayer. Asking God to make you perfect in His love will enable you to drive out fear in your life. God does not want us to be slaves to fear. Even though the unknown may seem frightening, God wants us to trust Him because nothing is unknown to Him. He is the God of the past, present and future.

Lord, You are the Alpha and the Omega, the beginning and the end. You know the future just as well as You know the past. As I trust in Your sovereignty, I pray that all of my fears will dissipate. As I prepare to give birth, there are many fears that will try to overpower my mind, but I pray for Your authority so that I may take every thought captive. You are a God of love and I pray for Your perfect love to drive out all fear from my mind. Please make me perfect in Your love. In Jesus' name I pray. Amen.

Month 6:
The Promise of Peace

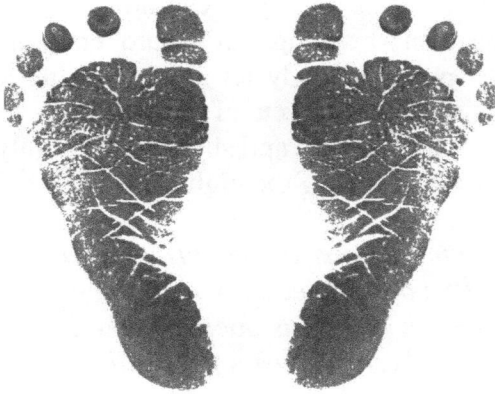

Day 1

Deuteronomy 33:12 *Let the beloved of the Lord rest secure in Him, for He shields them all day long.*

The whole process of pregnancy, from conception to delivery is amazing. What starts out as a tiny cell results in a living, breathing human being that resembles, to some degree, the parents who created him (her). It's incomprehensible how each phase falls into place- there are so many opportunities for problems to arise and so little you can do to prevent them. The anxiety can be overwhelming. It's hard enough to sleep and function with a pregnant body let alone with an anxious mind. There is only one true source of peace- God. He calls His beloved to rest secure in Him and shields us not only all day long, but also in the restlessness of the night.

Lord, I am anxious about this pregnancy. What if my baby is born with a birth defect? What if the pain is too much for me to bear? What if one of us doesn't make it? What if both of us don't make it? These are just a few of the "big worries" that I have Lord. I know that there is nothing I can do to guarantee a perfect baby and a perfect delivery and if I keep looking for a way I will drive myself crazy. Lord, there is only one way for me to have peace about this- to rest in You. Shield me from the dangers I may face in the day and keep my mind resting in Your peace throughout the night. In Jesus' name I pray. Amen.

Day 2

Numbers 6:25-26 *The Lord bless you and keep you; the Lord make His face shine upon you and be gracious to you; the Lord turn His face toward you and give you peace.*

As your baby floats around in your womb, you can seek the Lord's blessing for him (her). Each prayer and petition you make on behalf of your unborn child can bring you more peace. When we turn our hearts to the Lord, His face will shine upon us. How could anxiety have any power in the Light of the Lord? I can only imagine what having God's face shine upon me is like, but my best earthly comparison is the feeling that comes upon me just after I've been swimming in the ocean or a pool and I lay in the sun, letting it warm me (covered in lotion of course)! One day I will feel God's face shining upon me in heaven. But for now, I seek His peace by constantly turning toward Him.

Lord, I seek Your blessing for myself and my baby and I pray today for a healthy pregnancy, labor and delivery for both of us. Please keep us safe through each stage of this process. Shine Your face upon us and be gracious to us. Please turn Your face toward us and give us peace. Lord, I do not want to be wrought with anxiety. Help me to feel Your peace and abide in it. In Jesus' name I pray. Amen.

Day 3

Psalm 37:3-5a *Trust in the Lord and do good; dwell in the Lord and enjoy safe pasture. Delight yourself in the Lord and He will give you the desires of your heart. Commit your way to the Lord; trust Him.*

This psalm can encourage us at anytime in our lives but is especially helpful during the tumultuous time of pregnancy. Our truest peace can only come from trusting in God. God promises peace for us but in order to experience it there are a few things we must do ourselves. In order to enjoy the Lord's safe pasture we must dwell in Him and allow Him to dwell in us. This means opening our hearts and lives to Him. Delighting in the Lord means seeking Him and His ways and putting ourselves in synch with Him. When we open ourselves up to the Holy Spirit and allow Him to fill us, the will of God will supersede our own will. His desires will become our desires.

Lord, I look to You during this time for safety. Help me to completely trust in You and Your ways. Lord, I want to dwell in You so I can be safe and peaceful during this pregnancy. I empty myself out so that You can fill me. With Your help I say goodbye to my fears and worries and hello to trusting in You for peace. I may need to empty myself out everyday, maybe even every hour or every minute, so that the fears of the enemy will have no power in my mind. Lord, fill me with the Holy Spirit so that I may delight in You and please transform the desires of my heart to mirror Yours. In Jesus' name I pray. Amen.

Day 4

Psalm 55:22a *Cast all your cares on the Lord and He will sustain you.*

Worry is truly the work of Satan. When our minds take off on a whirlwind of uncontrollable anxiety, we are under Satan's power. Our God is the God of peace. He does not want our minds and our bodies to fall victim to the overwhelming stress that accompanies worry. When so much of life is out of control, as most of it is, we often turn away from God and start the "worry spin." What God wants us to do, as we acknowledge our lack of control, is to turn to Him. In our minds, peace can be improbable, even impossible, but turning to God and away from ourselves enables us to experience peace. Casting our cares on God takes the power of worry away from Satan and we no longer expose ourselves to its stress or depression. God is our only source of peace and His peace transcends all understanding (Philippians 4:7).

Lord, being an expectant mother can be worrisome. How can I keep but thinking of all the things that can go wrong? There is nothing I want more than a healthy baby and a safe delivery, but my thoughts keep turning to worry. I know I have little control over my situation and I start to play the "what if" game. Lord, remind me that my worry is sin. I confess it to You today and I cast all my cares upon You- asking You to sustain me. I know that I may have to pray this prayer daily, even hourly but I know that You are the source of all peace and I ask You to bless me with Your peace today. In Jesus' name I pray. Amen.

Day 5

Psalm 85:8 *I will listen to what the Lord will say; He promises peace to His people, His saints- but let them not return to folly.*

The Lord promises peace to His people and that peace surely includes pregnant people. Experiencing God's peace involves listening to what He says. Taking time to pray, meditate and listen to God will help to relieve our fears. Casting our fears upon Him involves engaging in a conversation with Him (and remember, a conversation is two-sided). Peace comes from opening up to God and waiting and listening for His response. Sometimes this can be hard. First of all, finding time to be still is difficult and will become nearly impossible once the baby arrives. Once we find time to talk to God we also have to make time to listen. If you're like me, centering your mind to be still is nearly impossible. I have the hardest time keeping my thoughts at rest. But I know that as my mind constantly wanders, God's voice becomes more difficult to hear. In Psalm 46:10, God beckons us to be still and know that He is God. It is only when we are still that we can enable ourselves to experience, not only the other side of the conversation, but also, God's miraculous peace.

Lord, I have so many concerns about this pregnancy and I look to You as the Author of Peace. I know that You promise peace to Your people and that peace comes from taking time to listen to You. Lord, I'm asking You, not to help me "find time" for You, but to help me make You my first priority. I want to love You, my God, with all my heart, all my mind and all my strength, but I get so distracted by life in the world. Lord, please show me how to be still because I have a great desire to hear You and experience Your peace. In Jesus' name I pray. Amen.

Day 6

Psalm 95:6-7 *Come, let us bow down in worship, let us kneel before the Lord our Maker, for He is our God and we are the people of his pasture, the flock under his care.*

When we are worshiping the Lord, we have no choice but to experience His peace. When we feel anxious about life, looking to God in worship enables us to block our worries. Focusing our mind's attention on the glory of God will leave no room for the enemy to produce and multiply doubt. Bowing down in worship enables us to acknowledge God's sovereignty and shifts our focus from our own worries to God's awesome glory. God is our maker and as His creation, we can experience His peace by bowing down in acknowledgement of His power and bringing glory to His name through worshiping Him in spirit and in truth.

Lord, I kneel down and bow my head to You today. I worship You as my Lord and Creator. You have given me life and given me the life of my baby and I praise You for both of these creations. You are the perfect Author of Life and Shepherd of Your children. I put both of our lives in Your hands- knowing that that's where they've come from and where they will remain. You are perfect peace and I ask that You would bestow that peace upon me today. In Jesus' name I pray. Amen.

Day 7

Psalm 119:76 *May Your unfailing love be my comfort, according to Your promise to Your servant.*

The closest thing we have to experiencing unfailing love on a human level is the term "unconditional love." Although those of us with pets might use them as a great example of unconditional love, it's also the way that parents describe their love for children. Hopefully, our love for our children is not based on conditions. And although our love, at its best may be unconditional, it is not unfailing. Our humanity can cause our love to fail; lack of patience, time, emotion and the like can leave our child feeling that our love is less than perfect. However, this never happens with God's love. His love for us is so unfailing that we can rest in it for our comfort. We love our children and want the best for them. God's love for us is similar, but it is also so much larger, more intense and absolutely perfect in nature.

Lord, I thank You for loving me with a perfect and unfailing love even though I am imperfect in so many ways. Although this life and this pregnancy may be difficult, I know that Your love will surround my situation and enable me to find comfort in You. Through all the difficulties that this world offers, Your love for me, which enables all things to work for good, will be my comfort. In Jesus' name I pray. Amen.

Day 8

Psalm 121:7-8 *The Lord will keep you from all harm- He will watch over your coming and going both now and forever more.*

As the Lord watches over our "coming and going" His provision becomes a duality. Initially, coming and going allude to daily routine: going out and coming home. God watches over our every move. Any harm that may come to us during our stay here on earth is directly under the Lord's watch and can therefore be used to achieve a greater good for His divine purpose. However, God is also present when we make our two most defining moves: our entrance into and exit out of life on earth. With God's promise in this psalm, you can also be sure that the Lord will be with your baby both as he (she) enters this world and as he (she) leaves it someday for the next.

Lord, I pray now for a blessing over my baby's "coming" into this world. I ask that You would watch over this grand entrance and keep my baby from all harm. I ask that Your presence would be so strong in our lives that we would never question Your protection. Please protect my child in this coming and in all his (her) comings and goings now, at the time of birth, throughout his (her) life and forevermore. In Jesus' name I pray. Amen.

Day 9

Proverbs 14:26 *He who fears the Lord has a secure fortress and for his children it will be a refuge.*

When we allow fear to take over our minds, we are allowing Satan to steal the peace that God gives us. Our lack of trust in Him enables fear to gain control. However, when our fear is of the Lord, we can experience fear in a positive way. Fear of the Lord enables us to establish a proper relationship with God in a reverent way. In the book of Proverbs, we see that fearing God also secures us. It is the relationship that we forge with God that gives us security in our lives and can then be transferred as a refuge to our children. Parents who have a God-fearing mindset prepare a safe place for their children's future.

Lord, I thank You for providing a secure fortress for me and a refuge for my children. Facing the unknown, especially the unknown of pregnancy, can be overwhelming, even frightening at times. I take comfort in knowing that You promise to be my protection. Lord, please help me to reverently fear You as the powerful God that You are. I want my relationship with You to be strong enough to provide a secure fortress for me and a refuge for my baby. Thank You Lord for being my Protection and my Provision. In Jesus' name I pray. Amen.

Day 10

Isaiah 26:3 *You will keep in perfect peace him whose mind is steadfast because he trusts in You.*

The Lord promises perfect peace to those who trust in Him. In so many situations in life, we must admit to a lack of power. Though we may try, there are innumerable instances in life that are simply outside the realm of our control. When we focus on our lack of power, we give fear a foot hold in our mind. However, when we shift our focus from all that we cannot do to all that our Lord can do, our fears will quickly be extinguished. Firmly fixing our thoughts upon God's awesome power, provision and protection will give us opportunity to experience His perfect peace.

Dearest Lord, I thank You for providing me with Your perfect peace. I come before You today surrendering my life to Your control. I've tried to control everything about my life and this pregnancy and I have come short. I turn to You now, knowing that Your perfect will for my life is to rest in Your peace. Help me to be steadfast in seeking Your peace so that fear will have no power in my mind both during this pregnancy and throughout my life. In Jesus' name I pray. Amen.

Day 11

Isaiah 40:11 *He tends his flock like a shepherd; He gathers the lambs in his arms and carries them close to his heart; he gently leads those that have young.*

Sometimes the idea of peace is just that- an idea. It may seem distant to us because it's intangible. However, God provides us with the perfect image of His peace. In Isaiah 40, God is portrayed as the perfect Shepherd, caring not only for the sheep but also for their lambs. Experiencing God's peace is made easier when we picture ourselves as sheep under His direct care, and becomes even clearer when we imagine our "lambs" in the arms of Jesus. Our young are kept close to His heart as they rest in His embrace- there is no other place of greater peace.

Lord, You are my perfect shepherd. Please care for me, Your sheep. I am only able to rest peacefully because I know that You will take care of me and my baby. Please hold my lamb in Your arms and lead me as I care for my young. Carry my baby close to Your heart and help each of us to be consoled by Your perfect peace. Thank You for the care that You give Your flock and for enabling us to be its restful members. In Jesus' name I pray. Amen.

Day 12

Isaiah 49:10 *The Lord who has compassion on them will guide them beside springs of water.*

Not only is God our shepherd, but He is also our guide, if we allow Him to be. In this verse, God is guiding His people to springs of water where they can be comforted from thirst and relax in peace. He is compassionate and sensitive to all of our needs and provides for us in every way. For each thirst, He will provide a spring of water. Lifting our "thirsts" or needs to Him will enable us to be at peace with them. When we surrender the anxiety we have about our lack of power, God, in His mighty power, will fill our minds with His perfect peace.

Lord, I pray for You to guide me to "springs of water" in my life. I may not be dehydrated from a lack of H_2O but my mind is presently dry of peace. I pray that You will guide me in how to refresh my mind with Your perfect peace. I know You are the ultimate source of peace and I surrender my anxiety to You today, just as I did yesterday and as I might have to do again tomorrow. Thank You for giving me the opportunity to never thirst again. In Jesus' name I pray. Amen.

Day 13

Isaiah 49:15 *Can a mother forget the baby at her breast and have no compassion on the child she has borne? Though she may forget, I will not forget you. See I have engraved you on the palms of my hands.*

In order to give us a sense of how strong God's love is for us, He has given mothers an intense love for their children. This love, though similar is a human comparison and, as we know humanity can fail. And so, God assures us that He is unfailing. His love for us is even stronger than the most intense love that we can experience in human relationships. What could be more assuring to expectant mothers than God engraving us on His palms? We are His and our unborn babies are His and living this truth will surely bring peace into our lives.

Lord, I thank You for giving us a peek at the intensity of Your love by giving us children to love. I thank You for this baby and I pray that I would be able to love him (her) the way You want me to. I praise You for engraving us on the palms of Your hands and I ask that we would always feel as close to You as we really are. Help me to see this experience from an eternal perspective and enable me to rest in Your perfect peace. In Jesus' name I pray. Amen.

Day 14

Isaiah 66:12a *I will extend peace to her like a river and the wealth of nations like a flowing stream.*

In this verse in Isaiah, the Lord promises to extend His peace to His people "like a river." With just a quick read, this seems like a strange simile to me. First of all, there are many things I can think of that are more peaceful, in my opinion, than a river. I know a river could be peaceful on a calm, sunny day, but I've also seen very rapid rivers. Once I widened my viewpoint from looking at a river and seeing how it's peaceful to looking at God's peace through the medium of a river, this verse began to make more sense. Rivers are strong, large powerful and life-sustaining. Similarly, God's peace is strong enough, large enough, and powerful enough to sustain us from the stronghold of anxiety. Rivers are also the source of flowing streams, which are connected to the main river. We, as Gentiles are connected to God's chosen people. He provides all of us with His miraculous peace.

Lord, I praise You for Your strength and Your power. I thank You for offering me a peace that has the same qualities. Your peace will enable me to overcome any anxiety that may creep into my mind. You have designed this world to reflect Your glory. Please let me experience Your peace like a river. Overflow and consume me with Your peace so that anxiety will have no place in my mind. In Jesus' name I pray. Amen.

Day 15

Isaiah 66:13 *"As a mother comforts her child, so will I comfort you," says the Lord.*

There are many techniques that we can use to comfort our newborns. Rocking, walking, jiggling, patting and singing are often the most popular because they come to us naturally. Newborns' instinct to sucking can also be comforted with pacifiers, which can be controversial. My first baby used one for close to a year, and my second was just never interested in one. I've also heard stories of parents running vacuum cleaners to calm their baby by replicating the noises of the womb. One universal comfort agent that I learned in the hospital is swaddling. This is an ancient technique that is very much applicable today. Folding a blanket tightly around a newborn helps recreate the closeness the baby experienced for the previous nine months. Although these are not the techniques that God uses with His children, He does comfort us in many other ways. The Holy Spirit is the great Comforter and will relieve any anxiety we lift up to Him.

Lord, I pray that I will be able to comfort my baby. Please enable my baby to feel at peace in my arms. Lord, please help me provide a peaceful environment for my baby. I praise You for the comfort You offer to Your people. I ask the Holy Spirit to renew peace in my heart today. Please relieve me from all anxiety and help me to remain calm as I provide comfort for my little one. In Jesus' name I pray. Amen.

Day 16

Jeremiah 24:6 *"My eyes will watch over them for their good,"* *says the Lord.*

The Lord is always watching over His people. His purposes for our lives are always good. However, God's goodness needs to be viewed from God's perspective. He watches over us because He wants the best for our lives, but when God is watching, He can see our lives in their eternity. He saw the beginning, He sees the end. This is sometimes difficult for us as humans because as we experience our lives, we only have knowledge of the moment we're in. We think how can this pain be "good"? How can this tragedy be "good"? Every occurrence in our lives, no matter how painful, is there to produce a greater outcome that God considers "good," and that could not happen without the pain. Think of it like a stone being thrown into a pond, where we can only see the stone, but God can see each ripple, each outcome, each effect of every occurrence, pain included. When a farmer prunes the branches of a vine to produce more fruit, the cutting doesn't necessarily cause the tree pain, but when God prunes our lives to produce fruit, we are susceptible to pain. And this pruning, this pain is more tolerable when we allow ourselves to feel His eyes watching over us and providing for goodness in the eternity of our lives.

Lord, I thank You for Your eyes. Thank You for watching over me and caring about the goodness of my life. I may not always feel like praising and thanking You for the painful situations in my life, but knowing that they are there to produce fruit makes the pain a bit easier to tolerate. I thank You Lord for Your goodness and know that You will watch over my baby for his (her) good. Please help me remember Your love for my child as he (she) goes through the pruning process too. In Jesus' name I pray. Amen.

Day 17

Ezekiel 34:12 *As a shepherd looks after his scattered flock when he is with them, so will I look after my sheep.*

In this verse, the prophet Ezekiel also describes the relationship between God and His people with the metaphor of a shepherd and his sheep. We are the Lord's sheep and are in His care. This illustration can be seen throughout the Old and New Testaments. What I find most interesting in this description is that even though the shepherd is with the sheep, they are still "scattered." Many times in pregnancy and even in life, we seem "scattered" either physically or mentally. We forget things, are distracted, we feel pulled in many directions, we may be tired or feeling apart from God. However, this verse assures us that even though we may feel scattered, God is still with us. We are never separated from His love and care. He looks after us as a perfect shepherd and by looking back to Him for comfort and protection, we can experience His perfect peace.

Lord, I am so glad You are my Shepherd. Thank You for looking out for me and for reuniting me with You when I feel "scattered." There are so many times when I feel alone and overwhelmed but I know that when I focus on being in Your care, I can rest peacefully. Please keep me and my baby in Your perfect care and peace. Remind me that I am always under Your watchful and caring eyes so that I will be able to face and overcome any anxiety in life. In Jesus' name I pray. Amen.

Day 18

Matthew 6:8 *"Your Father knows what you need before you ask him," Jesus replied.*

This verse can be simultaneously comforting and confusing. Knowing that our Father already knows what we need before we ask provides us with an awesome sense of security. If God already knows our needs then we have no need to worry. He will provide for them. The question that then arises is, if God already knows what we're going to ask Him for, why bother Him with prayer? Lifting our needs up to God in prayer opens direct lines of communication between God and His people. When we pray, we are responding to God's calling on our hearts. Of course God can provide for us without prayer, but He has established prayer as a means of communication. He loves to hear from His children and respond to their needs. God is the true author of prayer. When we allow His will to be our desire, our prayers become more effective.

Lord, I praise You today for knowing my needs and for caring about them. Your knowledge is not bound by time. You are omniscient. Thank You for caring about my needs and meeting them. Help me to rest in Your care so that I can be free from the restraints of anxiety. Please meet all of my physical and emotional needs during this pregnancy. In Jesus' name I pray. Amen.

Day 19

Matthew 6:34 *"Therefore, do not worry about tomorrow, for tomorrow will worry about itself."*

As your pregnant body grows with each "tomorrow," you may often find yourself anxious for your physical state. How can I possibly grow any larger? How can my stomach stretch any further? You may also worry about the big "tomorrow," the day of delivery. How will I survive the pain of labor? Will my baby be healthy? And there are also the concerns we may have for all of the "tomorrows" we will have with our babies. Will I be a good mother? Will I collapse from a lack of sleep? Anxiety about the future can be overwhelming. When we stay focused on each day and its concerns we can avoid being overcome by anxieties about the future.

Lord, I do not want to be a slave to worry. Please help me to lift each anxious thought up to You and surrender my concerns to Your will. Help me change each anxious thought into a prayer and let my prayers become a blanket of peace. Lord, I know that You want the best for my unborn baby and I ask that Your perfect will would be done in both of our lives. In Jesus' name I pray. Amen.

Day 20

Matthew 11:28 *"Come to me all who labor and are heavy laden and I will give you rest.*

Who better to be described as "labored and heavy laden" than an expectant mother? There's a very good reason why the process of giving birth is called labor- it's hard work! And, gaining twenty-five pounds or so will certainly make you feel "heavy laden." When you encounter the physical and emotional stress and anxiety that all expectant women face, there are many places you can go to try and find rest. You can seek physical rest on the couch or in bed, with your feet soaking or elevated and with the help of a heating pad or an ice pack. You can seek emotional rest through listening to classical music or reading. But true relief, both physical and emotional can only come from the true source- the love of Jesus Christ. When we look to our Lord for comfort, rest and peace, we will always find respite.

Lord, I praise You for being the ultimate source of rest in my life. There are so many times when I feel physical and emotional stress. I'm carrying around extra weight and it's taking a toll on my body. Not only is my body changing daily, but I am facing a huge change in my life. Whether this is my first baby or not doesn't matter. Each new life will bring about immense change, not just in my life, but in every life my child will affect. Lord, please help me to remember that Your love is the true source of comfort and in You I can find true peace. In Jesus' name I pray. Amen.

Day 21

John 10:28-29 *Jesus replied, "No one can snatch them out of my hand. My Father, who has given them to me, is greater than all; no one can snatch them out of my Father's hand. I and the Father are one."*

As Jesus is talking with His disciples in this verse, He explains to them that we, His children, have been given to Him by His Father. He then goes on to describe His deity, explaining that He and His father are one. This is a complex passage but it has a simple application to the lives of both an expectant woman and her unborn child. Both you and your baby belong to the Father. We are in His total care and there is no one, no event, nothing that can "snatch" us away. As we walk with Him, whatever happens to us will be part of His will. Every situation in our lives is there to bring about His perfect will for our lives and this is certainly one of them. Resting in His protection will enable us to experience His peace.

Lord, I thank You so much for giving me and my child to Your Son. I trust that He will care for us and that nothing will be able to thwart His protection. I know that even though we may experience hardships, You will use every difficulty to bring about Your will for us on earth, just as You do in heaven. Jesus, please keep us resting in Your loving hands and perfect peace. In Your name I pray. Amen.

Day 22

John 14:27 *"Peace I leave you; my peace I give you. I do not give to you as the world gives. Do not let your heart be troubled. Do not be afraid."*

God's peace is clearest as it is expressed in this verse. The Lord Jesus assures us that He will give the peace we so greatly desire. His desire is for our hearts to be free from fear. In this world we will experience troubles but we do not have to let those experiences leave us troubled. We can rest in the glorious peace that God gives us. Jesus' desire is for us to be filled with His gift of peace. He is the perfect and only true source of peace. Any peace we try to get from the world, any "relaxing" techniques we may try can only be temporary and as such, pale in comparison to the lasting and overwhelming peace that comes from experiencing the love of Christ.

Lord Jesus, I praise You for Your peacefulness. Thank You for offering Your perfect peace to me. You are the supreme gift giver. I know that Your kingdom is in heaven and as we live in this imperfect world, we will experience troubles. Please remind me that Your peace will keep me from being overwhelmed by these troubles. As I am now experiencing pregnancy and I face labor, delivery and motherhood, I ask that You would fill me with Your peace. In Jesus' name I pray. Amen.

Day 23

John 16:33 *"I have told you these things so that in me you may have peace. In this world you will have trouble. But take heart! I have overcome the world."*

Jesus is the one true source of peace that we can turn to when we have trouble. As Jesus tells us, troubles will come in this world and may often come during pregnancy, labor and delivery. These troubles, along with all of the difficulties of the world have already been overcome by Jesus. And it is through Him that you will be able to have peace through the difficulties of your pregnancy. When you are nauseous or exhausted, you can turn to Him for peace. When you are experiencing discomfort or outright pain, you can turn to Him for peace. As your water breaks and your labor pains begin, you can turn to Him for peace. Jesus did not go through the exact same experience, but He certainly knows physical and emotional pain and He overcame that pain for us freely so that we may experience His peace forever.

Lord, as my body changes with each day of pregnancy, I turn to You for peace. I know that You have overcome all of the difficulties of this world and it is through that power that You are able to offer peace to me. As the troubles I face during this pregnancy make me anxious, I can turn to You, knowing that You will not fail to relieve me from all anxiety. Please give me peace about each physical and emotional obstacle that I may face in the next few months. I praise You for triumphing over the troubles of this world and I rest in Your promise of peace. In Jesus' name I pray. Amen.

Day 24

Romans 8:6b *The mind controlled by the Spirit is life and peace.*

Anxiety originates and exists in our mind. When we enable our uncertainty to control our thoughts we succumb to the stress of anxiety. In order to battle anxiety, we need to engage in a mind war. In order to be at peace, our mind must be controlled by the Holy Spirit. When we start feeling anxious we may try to block those thoughts with our will power. This may work for a short period, but a mind that is truly at peace is one that has surrendered to the power of the Holy Spirit. Being filled with the Holy Spirit involves asking and seeking. Starting out each day with a prayer to God asking to be filled with the power of the Holy Spirit will certainly cause our anxiety to step aside and surrender the territory of our minds to the power of God's peace.

Lord, I come before You humbled and seeking. My mind is wrought with anxiety and I need Your Holy Spirit to come upon me and fill me with peace. I don't want to be anxious for anything, but as I feel anxiety growing, I ask that You, in Your awesome power would sweep it away with true peace. Live in me so that I can live for You. Help me to see my life and this pregnancy through spiritual eyes. I love You and want more of You and less of me as I grow each day. In Jesus' name I pray. Amen.

Day 25

2 Corinthians 1:3-4 *Praise be to the God and Father of Our Lord Jesus Christ, the Father of compassion and the God of all comfort, who comforts us in all our troubles.*

When we face trouble in our lives, we can cope with it in a number of ways. Some people find comfort at the bottom of a glass, others at the bottom of a bag of potato chips, neither of which is recommended for an expectant mother. Whether your troubles are focused around pregnancy or not, comfort from them and the anxiety they cause, is best found in our heavenly Father. Comfort that the world offers is weak at best and in excess can be detrimental. But the comfort that God offers is true, is everlasting and is offered to us in love. Our God is the God of all comfort, He can relieve you from all troubles, especially the ones you may face as the days of labor and delivery approach.

Lord, like Your servant Paul, I praise You today for being my Father. Praise be to You, the God and Father of Our Lord Jesus Christ, the Father of compassion and the God of all comfort, who comforts us in all our troubles. Thank You for being my Father and for supplying me with infinite and eternal comfort. Please let Your comfort cleanse my mind from all anxiety. As my due date approaches, I can feel my anxiety growing. I look to You now for the comfort that You offer for all troubles and I seek Your peace as I prepare for this awesome event. In Jesus' name I pray. Amen.

Day 26

2 Thessalonians 3:16 *Now may the Lord of peace Himself give you peace at all times and in every way. The Lord be with all of you.*

Our God is the Lord of peace. He is true peace. If we are to experience the glory of that peace, we need to experience Him. When Paul writes to the Thessalonians in this verse, he prays that the Lord would be with them. When we make a similar prayer, asking the Lord to be with us, we will keep our minds from having the opportunity to stir up anxiety. Having God's peace means having God- having Him in our daily thoughts and through our struggles and as the center of our lives. Paul tells us to pray unceasingly (1 Thessalonians 5:17). If we heed his advice, we are guaranteed to experience God's peace at all times and in every way. When we transform our anxious thoughts into prayers, our anxiety is smothered by the power of our prayers.

Lord, please be with me today. I know that if I let You into my heart You will fill it with Your peace. I want to pray unceasingly, but it's so hard. Everything in this world is so distracting- even the good things, like kids! Help me to remember You at each possible moment. Let me praise You when I experience joy and turn to You with my anxious thoughts. I know the more I turn to You, the more I will be comforted. Help me to pull away from the thoughts of this world and set my thoughts on things above. Lead me and guide me. In Jesus' name I pray. Amen.

Day 27

Colossians 3:15 *Let the peace of Christ rule in your hearts, since, as members of one body you were called to peace.*

Christ wants to be King of our hearts. He wants to rule our minds, hearts and bodies. But as humans, we are prideful. We think, either consciously or unconsciously, "I can do this myself." And when we battle against Him, when we let our pride win, we are really losing. Keeping Christ from reigning in our hearts keeps us from experiencing His peace. Christ wants to live in us so that we can take part in all that He has to offer. However, He won't just come in and take over. We need to surrender to Him. We need to refuse giving power to our prideful selves. We need to die to our selves daily, to our pride and our selfishness and our greed, so that Christ can take over the throne of our hearts. It is only when He reigns that we will be able to fully take part in His perfect peace.

Lord, I know that You have called me to peace and that Your will for this pregnancy is for it to be a time of peace. Help me Lord to rest in Your peace. Please help me to surrender myself to You so that You can reign in my heart with peacefulness. When my pride takes over, I am removed from You. My humanness desires to be in control of every aspect of this pregnancy, but I know that is impossible. That conflict is what causes such unrest. Lord, I come before You now with a humbleness in my heart that welcomes You in. Please rule over my heart and my pregnancy so that I can abide in Your peace. In Jesus' name I pray. Amen.

Day 28

Ephesians 2:14a *For He Himself is our peace.*

Peace, in its most effective and enduring form comes from one source: Christ Jesus. So, as logic would have it, if we want to get peace, we have to get Christ. When we set our thoughts upon Him, we allow His peace to rule in our hearts. There are a number of ways to "get" Him in our lives. We can meditate upon His word or call out to Him in prayer. We can picture ourselves resting in His loving arms or reading His Word. Just asking for the Holy Spirit to fill us will certainly enable us to experience peace. Call out to the Holy Spirit at the height of anxiety, or better yet, as soon as those ugly thoughts begin to stir up. God's peace is available to us, infinite and priceless. All we have to do is seek it.

Lord, I praise and thank You for offering Your peace to me. I know that You are the one, true source of peace. I want Your peace in my life more than anything else. I know that without it, I will be a wreck during the rest of this pregnancy. I want to enjoy this time and to anticipate this birth while experiencing Your peace. I call out to You today and ask the Holy Spirit to fill my mind, body and soul. Please consume me with Your peace so that anxiety will have no room to plant its ugly seeds of doubt and worry. I want all of the glory of this pregnancy to exalt Your name. In Jesus' name I pray. Amen.

Day 29

Philippians 4:7 *Do not be anxious about anything, but in everything, by prayer and petition make your requests known to God. And the peace of God, which transcends all understanding, will guard your hearts and minds in Christ Jesus.*

In this verse, Paul is writing God's message to the Christians in Philippi, encouraging them during anxious times. But that message wasn't for them alone. It is a loving message from God to His children, there and then and here and now. God wants us to know that we do not need to be anxious, that there is a remedy to the queasiness of anxiety. When we begin to worry, we are to pray and ask God for relief and His peace will prevail. God isn't guaranteeing that He will answer our prayers the way we would like Him to; He might or He might not. However, there are two guarantees that He does offer. First, whatever God does to answer our prayers will be what is best for us in each situation and what will bring glory to His name, both of which are always His will. The second guarantee is that however God's will plays out in our lives, easy or hard, it will be accompanied by His peace, as soon as we ask.

Lord, I pray today for Your peace. I bring my prayers and petitions to You, with slight suggestions about how I would like them answered. I am more vulnerable to anxiety while I am pregnant because I so desire the best for my baby. Just as I want the best for my baby, I know that You also want the best for me, yet I need to understand that Your best will not always match my plans and may not be the easiest route. Help me to submit to Your will and Your plan. I surrender this baby to Your will today. I trust Your love and the power of Your peace and ask You to fill my heart with them today. In Jesus' name I pray. Amen.

Day 30

1 Peter 5:7 *Cast all your anxieties on Him because He cares for you.*

When I think of casting, the first thing that comes to mind is fishing. Although I am not a big fan of fishing, I do like to imagine myself removing my anxious thoughts from my mind, attaching them to a hook and hurling them out to sea. That is also what God has in mind for our anxiety. He does not want us to be burdened by worry- you have enough to experience and plan for as an expectant mother. We don't have time to play games with the enemy's toys. God cares about us and although He created us, as humans, to be susceptible to worry, He did not abandon us. He will take our worry and turn it into peace. Just cast the line.

Lord, I praise and thank You for caring so much about me and my baby. I know that You want the best for us and an anxious spirit is certainly not the best. I ask You to show me how to bait my line with worry and cast my anxiety on You. In Your awesome power I know that You will fill my heart and mind with peace. There are so many wonderful things to think about as an expectant mother, including the miracle of life growing inside me, I do not want to be trapped into wasting my thoughts on worries. Please free me from anxiety and enable me to walk in Your peacefulness. In Jesus' name I pray. Amen.

Month 7:
The Promise of Strength

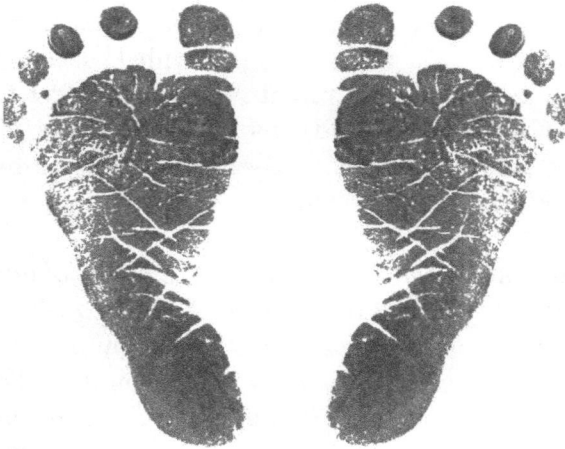

Day 1

2 Samuel 22:33 *It is God who arms me with strength and makes my way perfect.*

From the moment you find out you are pregnant until the moment your grown child moves out of the house (and maybe not even then) you will need God's strength. At first it may just be physical but soon it will also become mental and emotional. Where does the kind of superhero strength that is needed to grow and raise a child come from? From God. God arms you with strength and when you align your life with His will, your ways will become perfect. They might not seem perfect to a human living in an imperfect world, but in God's eyes a life lived according to His plan will not only be strengthened by Him, but can be nothing less than perfect.

Lord, I know that You will be with me through every step of this pregnancy. From the moment I see two blue lines on a pregnancy test to the moment I hold my baby in my arms, You will be there, strengthening me. I also know that You will not depart from me as we're wheeled out of the hospital doors. Raising this baby is also going to take the superhuman strength that only You can provide. From the sleepless nights of infant feedings to the sleepless nights of teenage driving, I know that I can rely on You to strengthen me as a parent. In Jesus' name I pray. Amen.

Day 2

1 Chronicles 12-13b *You are the ruler of all things. In Your hands are the strength and power to exalt and give strength to all. Now our God we give You thanks and praise Your glorious name.*

One of the first symptoms of pregnancy is nausea. Some women experience it even before they miss their period. Wrongly named "morning sickness," this nausea can start at any time throughout the day and can last well into the afternoon and evening hours. Some women are not affected by this at all; others find themselves running to the bathroom several times a day. When you become pregnant, the food you eat is quickly transformed into glucose to "feed" the baby. This causes low blood sugar which in turn can cause nausea. Pregnancy hormones can also cause you to be nauseous. Nausea is heightened when you have an empty stomach, so it may help to eat small meals throughout the day, snack on crackers or toast, especially before getting out of bed, avoid fatty, fried or spicy foods. And keep in mind that this condition usually goes away after the first trimester.

Lord, I praise You for being the ruler of all things. I know that in Your hands You have the power to give strength to all. I ask that You would give me that strength today. As I'm feeling nauseous or just run down Lord, I pray that I would be strengthened through Your power. As my body struggles with changing hormones and low blood sugar, strengthen it so that I can continue being healthy. Please take this morning sickness away as soon as possible and help me to function with it while it lasts. In Jesus' name I pray. Amen.

Day 3

1 Chronicles 16:11 *Look to the Lord and His strength; seek His face always. Remember the wonders He has done, His miracles and the judgments He pronounced.*

Another symptom of first trimester pregnancy is fatigue. You will just plainly feel exhausted. Growing another human being saps your energy, but fatigue is also caused by the hormone progesterone. Rest is very important to your physical health and you should take advantage of it now, while you're body can still find comfortable positions. If this is your first baby, you should really rejoice in your ability to nap during your free time because this will be your last chance! All subsequent pregnancies will be accompanied by the needs of your other children. So for now, let the housework go and rest while your baby grows!

Lord, I look to You and Your strength when I have none. As my body is changing with this pregnancy, I find myself very sleepy. I know that I can find rest in You, especially emotionally and mentally, but I also ask for physical rest. Please help me clear my schedule so that I can find time to give my body what it needs. Strengthen me during times of weakness when I can't rest and help me maintain a healthy body and growing environment for my baby. In Jesus' name I pray. Amen.

Day 4

2 Chronicles 32:7-8 *Be strong and courageous. Do not be afraid or discouraged because of the King of Assyria and the vast army with him, for there is a greater power with us than with him. With him is only the arm of flesh, but with us is the Lord our God to help us fight our battles.*

When we attempt to attain our strength from "flesh" or our bodies, we will often fail because our physical strength is limited by the frailty of our human bodies. This becomes obvious during pregnancy. No matter how much you want or try to be strong, sooner or later, you will find yourself restricted by the physical symptoms of pregnancy. You may be fatigued or nauseous or swollen. You may be restricted by constipation or a headache or back pain. These are the ways that your body responds to the dramatic changes of pregnancy. However, you should never feel overcome by these physical restrictions, because true strength does not come from the "arm of flesh" but from the Lord our God, who helps you fight, or overcome the physical battles of pregnancy.

Lord, I praise You for being the ultimate source of strength. You enable me to be strong and courageous. When I feel overwhelmed by the physical struggles of pregnancy, I pray that I would look to You as my source of strength. Help me resist feeling afraid or discouraged as I deal with all of these physical changes. Lord, I look to You knowing there is so much I am not able to do myself. Please give me the strength I need throughout the day and show me where to prioritize so I can get the most out of the energy I have left. In Jesus' name I pray. Amen.

Day 5

Psalm 29:11 *The Lord gives strength to His people; the Lord blesses His people with peace.*

Most of what weighs an expectant mother down is weight gain. Before your nine months is up, you will have gained anywhere from 25 to 35 pounds. You may feel that this becomes a burden on your back, knees and body in general. As you reach the latter months of pregnancy, you may find it difficult to move and almost impossible to get comfortable. This extra weight doesn't come just from the baby. Your little one will account for about 7 pounds. The rest comes from increased fluids, including amniotic fluid, an enlarged uterus, the placenta, stored protein and an increase in blood volume.

Lord, I want to pray right now for my weight gain. I have many food cravings now, but I want to make sure that as I gain weight, it is a healthy amount. I know that too much weight gain is not healthy for either of us. Help me control my weight gain so that I can create the best growing environment for my baby. Lord, please strengthen my body as it responds to these new pounds. Keep my back strong and if it is at all possible, help me to find a comfortable position for resting. In Jesus' name I pray. Amen.

Day 6

Psalm 46:1 *God is our refuge and our strength, an ever-present help in trouble.*

Some of the "trouble" you may face in pregnancy is going to be caused by uncontrollable emotions. Don't be surprised if you find yourself feeling euphoric and depressed in the same fifteen minutes. You may find yourself crying for no reason, anxious, fearful or even bursting out in laughter. Hormones from pregnancy can affect your central nervous system, leaving your emotions out of the realm of your control. Whatever emotions you experienced as part of premenstrual syndrome are only intensified by pregnancy. Any serious signs of depression should be discussed with your doctor, but the spectrum for normal pregnancy emotions is wide and it should be, your life is about to be changed forever.

Lord, please help me get some grip over my emotions. I don't want to feel like I'm carrying around a basket of emotions, reacting to whichever one happens to fall into my lap. Lord please give my mind strength as it experiences hormonal changes. When I think about everything that having this baby means I am ecstatic, afraid, frustrated, anxious and over excited. So many aspects of my life are going to change, please help me know how to handle this transformation. In Jesus' name I pray. Amen.

Day 7

Psalm 73:26 *My flesh and my heart may fail, but God is the strength of my heart and my portion forever.*

One way that you might be surprised to find your flesh "failing" during pregnancy is in the bowel department. This is not the most polite aspect of pregnancy to discus, but it does affect many women. One symptom is constipation. An increase in pregnancy hormones causes bowel movements to slow down. Combating constipation can be done with dietary changes such as the inclusion of prunes or bran. Drinking plenty of water may also help. But beware, the solutions you use to battle constipation may have an opposite affect and you might soon find yourself feeling gassy and bloated. It's really a no win situation. The best solution I've found is just to attempt to deal with each problem as it comes along. Stay hydrated and as active as possible and talk to your doctor if any of these symptoms become serious.

Lord, I believe that the most troublesome aspect of pregnancy is the discomfort. The physical difficulties can take many forms. Today I lift my digestive system up to You Lord. Please strengthen my flesh as it battles the hormones of pregnancy. Help me make effective dietary changes. Lord, I praise You for being the strength of my heart and my portion forever. Please help me to overcome the physical discomfort of this pregnancy. In Jesus' name I pray. Amen.

Day 8

Psalm 77:14 *You are the God who performs miracles, You display Your power among the peoples.*

One important aspect of prenatal health is movement. Being as fit as possible before, during and after labor will only make your pregnancy and recovery more manageable. Now, I'm not talking about weight loss, just fitness. The more apt you are to keep moving, the easier it will be to shed those post baby pounds. You will also find yourself with more energy and less stress if you make exercise part of your normal routine. Make sure you discuss any routine with your physician, but if you have a normal pregnancy any kind of moderate exercise such as walking, swimming, aerobics or yoga should only enhance your health.

Lord, there is nothing I desire more than a healthy pregnancy and a healthy baby. Help me choose an activity that will contribute to our health and show me how I can possibly fit it into my schedule. Lord, give me strength as I choose to put this large body into motion and bless my workout times. Protect me from injury or strains. Please display Your great power through every aspect of this pregnancy. In Jesus' name I pray. Amen.

Day 9

Psalm 89:13 *Your arm is endured with power; Your hand is strong, Your right hand exalted.*

As your pregnancy progresses, you will become familiar with the ultrasound process. I had at least 4 with each pregnancy. The first ultrasound, given at about 12 weeks was the most difficult and really took all of my strength to hold my bladder. You will be instructed to finish drinking anywhere from 32 to 64 ounces of fluid, depending on how far along you are. Since frequent urination is a normal symptom of pregnancy, this becomes a difficult feat! It also helps if your appointment is running on time. Your first ultrasound may be twofold; you may have the standard abdominal, and also a vaginal, where a transducer will be directly inserted. Hopefully, after the initial measurements are taken, you will be able to empty your bladder a little, to make you more comfortable. Holding a full bladder is the worst part of an ultrasound; seeing your baby is the best! This is such a great way to get a sneak peak of what your baby looks like. Some offices are offering 4D ultrasounds which enable you to get a really clear picture of your baby. By 16 weeks your technician might be able to tell the sex of your baby if you want to know. It can also reassure you of your baby's health. But remember that some information can be misleading. I know women whose ultrasounds didn't pick up the most serious of complications and I know women who had scares from ultrasound results and perfectly healthy babies.

Lord, I ask You to strengthen me during my ultrasound examinations, especially strengthen my bladder. Although this is not a painful procedure, it can be very uncomfortable. Lord I ask that You give the technician eyes to see any problems with my baby and the wisdom to know how to communicate this information to me. In the same way, I pray that there will be no unnecessary scares about the baby's health. This baby is Your child as much as it is mine and I want to have Your peace in knowing that he (she) is perfectly formed according to Your will. In Jesus' name I pray. Amen.

Day 10

Psalm 121:3 *The Lord will not let your foot slip- He who watches over you will not slumber.*

Sometimes, when you're pregnant, you can't help dealing with the same illness that the rest of the world does: allergies, colds, the flu, etc. However, oftentimes, you can no longer combat these illnesses with the same medications. Some medications may seem obvious to avoid, others not so much. One thing that surprised me, as I dealt with an aching back during pregnancy, was the inability to use a heating pad. Who would have thought? Other common medications to avoid include bismuth subsalicylate, commonly known as Pepto-Bismol®, as well as ibuprofen. Doctors have categorized medication based on studies that have determined their safeness. When medication is to be avoided, it's best to deal with common illnesses by getting rest, drinking plenty of fluids and using natural remedies like gargling with salt water, drinking orange juice and eating chicken noodle soup. Be sure to contact your physician with all of your medical questions.

Lord, I know that in my human body, I am susceptible to illness. As an expectant mother, I can't always use medication to relieve the symptoms. I pray that You would protect my body from illness and injury, especially while I am pregnant. Lord, if I do become susceptible to illnesses, I pray that I would have the strength to weather through them. Please help my doctor to be knowledgeable of what medications I can take and to advise me so that I can continue to have a healthy pregnancy. In Jesus' name I pray. Amen.

Day 11

Psalm 150:2 *Praise Him for His acts of power; praise Him for His surpassing greatness.*

Throughout your pregnancy you will be given many different kinds of tests. Some through blood others through urine. These are preventative, so that a potential problem, if found can be solved or dealt with as soon as possible. One of the first tests is a pap smear, where the doctor scrapes the inside of your cervix so the cells can be tested for cancer. You may also have blood tests for anemia and to determine your blood type. During your fourth month of pregnancy you will have an alpha-fetoprotein (AFP) test that will indicate the possibility of your baby having Down's Syndrome. And later on you will be tested to see if you've developed gestational diabetes. These tests can be stressful both in their procedures and results. If you're not fond of needles or you get a false positive on these tests, your stress levels will be heightened. With my first baby, I got a false positive for the AFP test. Even though the percentage of true positives is small, it's a scary situation. The results however were false because the laboratory had recorded the wrong week of pregnancy when they took the test. If these tests cause high levels of stress for any reason, I urge you to use that weakness to seek out God's strength. Look to the power of God and to His surpassing greatness.

Lord, I look to You as I undergo each of the many medical test of pregnancy. As an expectant mother I am trying to do the very best to ensure my baby will be healthy. But sometimes all of the testing can be stressful. I am weakened by the procedure: the insurance cards, the referrals, the waiting room, the needles. And I am weakened by the results: the false positives and the chance of a true positive. I ask You to take my weakness today and fill me with Your strength. Your acts of power and Your surpassing greatness are amazing. Please comfort me during these tests. In Jesus' name I pray. Amen.

Day 12

Isaiah 12:2 *Surely God is my salvation; I will trust and not be afraid. The Lord, the Lord is my strength and my song. He has become my salvation.*

As your pregnancy continues, you may begin to feel your stress levels rise accordingly. There are so many changes it's normal to feel a little overwhelmed. You may be anxious about your body's physical changes. Will you ever wear a bikini again? You may be worried about finances, returning or not returning to work, or preparing the nursery. Or you might be like me and stress over the health and development of your baby. These are all real concerns. But when they become more than concerns they can be detrimental to your health. Chronic stress can have a negative affect on your health. During my pregnancies, I found that I had little control over any of these issues and feeling stressful about them was a waste of time, energy and emotion. Trusting God to take away my fear helped me to see that He is my strength and my song and that He alone can save me from the weakness of anxiety.

Lord, I praise You for being my strength and my salvation. I lift this pregnancy up to You today. There are so many aspects of it that weaken me with fear and anxiety. Help me surrender that fear to You, knowing that You will provide all of the strength I need to deal with every concern I may have during this pregnancy. Show me how to lift every concern up to You before Satan has a chance to turn it into a paralyzing fear. I don't want my health to suffer because of unnecessary stress. Lord, I pray for Your strength and Your salvation. In Jesus' name I pray. Amen.

Day 13

Isaiah 40:26 *Lift your eyes and look to the heavens: Who created all these? He who brings out the starry host one by one and calls them each by name. Because of His great power and mighty strength not one of them is missing.*

Just think of the wonder that this verse brings to life when you apply it to your baby. The God you worship is the Lord. He created the heavens. He formed each star in the sky and He calls them by name. His infinite knowledge, care and love are not limited even by something as vast as the universe. Not one star is missing. Even the universe submits to the will of God. God's love is large enough to embody all of space and intimate enough to care about each molecule in it. His love for your baby is the same. He knows his (her) name even before you have chosen it. And it is through His power and mighty strength that your baby will enter this world.

Lord, I praise you for all that You are. I am so humbled to worship the Lord of the universe. You created something so vast as the heavens and so small as this infant inside me. And I know that every baby born is Your creation and Your gift. Lord, strengthen me as I attempt to care for this child. Father, help me to be a reflection of You as I parent him (her). Lord, I know that You knew my baby's name even before I did. I pray that throughout this pregnancy and this baby's life I would be able to keep in mind just how much you love him (her), even more than I do. In Jesus' name I pray. Amen.

Day 14

Isaiah 40:29-31 *He gives strength to the weary and increases the power of the weak. Even youths grow tired and weary and young men stumble and fall; but those who hope in the Lord will renew their strength.*

Some of the weariness of pregnancy can come in the form of indigestion. Commonly known as heartburn, this affliction affects many pregnant women, especially in the late months of expectancy. An old wives' tale might have you believe that a hairy baby is the cause for this suffering, but there is also a physical explanation. As your uterus grows, it begins to push up on your stomach, making food harder to digest. When there is not enough room for your food to move down, it can come back up, thus producing heartburn. Some relief can be found by avoiding fatty and greasy foods, drinking plenty of water and using an antacid such as Tums®, which will also provide you with extra calcium.

Lord, I praise You today for caring about my body and my physical needs. As this baby grows inside me, digesting food becomes more difficult and uncomfortable. I ask You to help me make healthy food choices and enable those choices to nourish my baby as he (she) grows and develops. Bless my body so that all parts of it, including the digestive system work properly. In Jesus' name I pray. Amen.

Day 15

Isaiah 45:24a *They will say of me, "In the Lord alone are righteousness and strength."*

Weight gain is a very important part of pregnancy. It mattered a lot to my doctors and it can take a physical and emotional toll on you as well. First of all, it's inevitable. Second of all, it doesn't just have to be in the general stomach area. It can be everywhere. Third of all, clothes can help. A healthy amount of weight gain is important, especially to obstetricians, and so, you should expect to be weighed at every doctor visit. If your self image has you down, try to remember that this is only a temporary state. Treating yourself to some new fashions can boost your emotions as well. Long gone are the days of maternity muumuus. Most department stores now carry a stylish and affordable line of maternity clothes.

Lord, please strengthen me as I grow. I don't want to be weighed down by weight gain. Strengthen my self-control so that I don't eat much more than I need to. Help me make healthy food choices. Lord, use everything I eat to nourish my baby. As my body grows, I know that some things, like seeing my feet in the shower, will become more and more difficult. Help me also to keep my spirit up as I grow. Show me how beautiful a pregnant body is. Let me see myself as You see me- a child of God. And Lord, help me to find some great deals on some cute fashions. In Jesus' name I pray. Amen.

Day 16

Isaiah 46:4 *I have made you and I will carry you; I will sustain you and I will rescue you says the Lord.*

Some of the most intense "sustaining" of my pregnancy came from backaches. At around the fifth month or so, you may notice an increase in weight gain, which is redistributed differently. Whether or not you notice it, this affects the way you sit, stand, walk and move in general. This compensation for the weight gain can put a strain on your back causing aches and pains. Your spine will also change to make space for the baby, thus causing additional muscle strain. I saw a chiropractor during my pregnancy to help with the pain I had when walking. Additional relief can come from sitting or laying down as often as possible, lifting as little as possible, and when necessary, lifting with your knees bent, using your leg muscles instead of your back. Sleep sideways with a pillow between your legs to eliminate extra pull on your spine and carry a small pillow with you when you are going to be sitting for long periods of time. You may even want to schedule professional massages on a regular basis. The relaxation alone may be enough to aid your aching back muscles.

Lord, I know that You have made me and You will carry me. As I carry this child, there is intense pressure on my back. My muscles ache and I am often in pain. Lord, I ask that You would continue to support me and sustain me during this pregnancy. Strengthen my back. Show me what positions will be most comfortable. Enable me to give my body ample rest. If I go to a chiropractor, please give him (her) the ability to safely adjust my back during pregnancy. Lord, bless my body as it goes through such tremendous physical changes. In Jesus' name I pray. Amen.

Day 17

Habakkuk 3:19 *The sovereign Lord is my strength; He makes my feet like the feet of a deer, He enables me to go on the heights.*

This prophet symbolically declared that the Lord made his feet like those of a deer with the idea that the Lord strengthened him to run faster and jump and climb higher. Although an expectant woman's feet do not become hooves, there are many podiatric changes in store. As your stomach grows, it will start to block your view of your feet, especially from a standing position. You may also find that your shoes don't fit anymore. Some women's feet grow a whole size during pregnancy. They might stay bigger or shrink back after delivery. The increase in size can also be credited to the retention of water or the expansion of foot joints, which is caused by hormones. Whatever the case, it is important to stay off your feet as much as possible, especially in the last trimester, and try to elevate them when you are lying down. Wear comfortable shoes whenever you can and avoid heels. Think comfort, your body will thank you.

Lord, please give me strength as my feet and ankles undergo changes during this pregnancy. I ask that You would enable me, not to go on the heights, but to just go on, on with my daily life. Let me get the things I need to do done and let me see what things I really need to do. Help me to listen to my body and to give it rest when it calls me to bed. Lord, protect my body through these changes. In Jesus' name I pray. Amen.

Day 18

1 Corinthians 2:3-5 *I came to you in my weakness and fear, with much trembling. My message and my preaching were not with wise, persuasive words, but with a demonstration of the Spirit's power, so that your faith might not rest on men's wisdom, but on God's power.*

In this past century, there was a time when doctors believed that the less women knew about pregnancy, the better off they were. Whatever you learned came from the stories of your mother and other women in your life. There were no such things as pregnancy books and Lamaze classes. Pregnancy was something to hide, as evidenced in 1950's maternity clothes styles. Knowledge of pregnancy has come a long way. Childbirth as the leading cause of death in women is no longer. The survival rates for both women and infants are higher than ever. Doctors have more knowledge about obstetrics and more tools to help them than ever before. Yet I believe that some expectant women are just as worried and just as weak before the labor and delivery process as ever. Our knowledge has increased immensely but our strength and our peace will not do the same until we place it where it will thrive- not in our own wisdom, but in God's power.

Lord, I pray for Your strength today. I like to rely on technology and the wisdom of the world to reassure me that everything will be all right, but I know from experience that this reassurance is fleeting. The only true strength comes from You, from Your power. I put my faith in You today, in Your love for me and for my baby, knowing that You will work out Your loving will in our lives as we journey through this process together. In Jesus' name I pray. Amen.

Day 19

2 Corinthians 12:9 *My grace is sufficient for you, for my power is made perfect in weakness.*

There is never a moment in our lives when we don't need God's strength. I pray for Him to give me strength every morning. But it seemed that when I was pregnant, I was seeking God's strength continually. Pregnancy left me in a weakened state. It was harder to move, harder to rest and harder to get comfortable. I needed God for energy, for stamina, for peace, both mental and physical. It was almost as if God was using this weakened state to bring me closer to Him. During labor and delivery, it was God's power that enabled my weakened body to give birth. My lack of strength gave God an outlet to make His power perfect in my life.

Lord, I pray to You today thanking You for Your amazing power. I know that my body is weak and especially during this pregnancy, there are so many times when I rely on You to strengthen me. Lord, please fill me with Your sufficient grace. As I face difficulty and weakness, I pray that Your perfect power will strengthen me. Help me also Lord to remember Your strength and Your power even when I don't seem to need them. When my body is healthy and I am peaceful and energized help me to continue to look to You as my Lord. In Jesus' name I Pray. Amen.

Day 20

2 Corinthians 12:10 *That is why, for Christ's sake, I delight in weakness…for when I am weak, then I am strong.*

Not many people I know delight in weakness. And as your pregnancy develops, you will find yourself in an increasingly weakened state. But what Paul is sharing here is that human weakness makes way for God's strength. What cannot be done alone, has to be done through Him. Humanness is limiting, but only so that Christ's power can be allowed to shine. Letting God be your strength will enable you to be truly strong. So while Paul is delighting in his weakness, what he is really saying is that he delights in the need for Christ because he knows that Christ's power is so much stronger than his could ever be.

Lord, because I am human I know that I am going to try. I am going to give it my all. Whenever I need to be strong I will use all of my self will to persevere. But hopefully that won't last long. In my head I know that the sooner I turn to You and ask You for Your strength and Your power, the better off I will be. Lord, as my pregnancy develops, my need for Your strength increases. Please use Your power to erase my weakness. Whatever I can't do alone, please help me to accomplish using Your strength. In Jesus' name I pray. Amen.

Day 21

Ephesians 1:19-20a *His incomparably great power is for us who believe. That power is like the working of His mighty strength, which He exerted in Christ when He raised Him from the dead.*

I like to do things independently. I really have trouble relying on other people to do things that I can usually do. But when I was pregnant I could not exert any strength in lifting things. There was so much I wanted to do on my own, but for fear of hurting myself or the baby, I would have to find someone else to do it. It really was a discipline to have to ask others for help. What if they didn't do things exactly how I would? But little by little as I got further along in pregnancy and now in motherhood, I have developed less trouble asking for help. Sometimes I have to wait longer than it would normally take me to do it, or have it done differently but I'm learning that there is only one person who should be in control of my life.

Lord, I praise You for the strength that You exhibited when You raised Christ from the dead. Your great strength has power even over death. Throughout this pregnancy I am in a weakened state. I can no longer use my strength to lift things or do any kind of strenuous activity that was so simple before. I have to rely on others and giving up control is difficult. Lord, I ask that You would help me see that You have true control over my life and that surrendering to You and asking others for help is Your will and, although it may be frustrating, is the safest option. In Jesus' name I pray. Amen.

Day 22

Ephesians 3:16 *I pray that out of His glorious riches He may strengthen you with power through His spirit in your inner being.*

Sometimes an expectant mother needs the most power in controlling emotions, especially those of irritation caused by the constant comments from other people. Everyone you see wants to know when you're due, how you're feeling and if you know what you're having. Some people will want to touch your belly (hopefully not many). You may hear plenty of jokes and even more advice. It may be that everyone means well, but people act differently around pregnant women. They say and do things that they wouldn't normally do. You're at an exciting stage in life and most of them just want to contribute in some way. Use God's power through the Holy Spirit to calm your inner being and show Christ's love.

Lord, I know that people mean well when they question and comment. They just want to show that they care about us. But sometimes it can be dreadfully annoying Lord. Please give me emotional strength to deal with the world right now. Help me react as You would, in a kind and loving way. Let me see them through Your eyes Lord. Strengthen me with Your power, through the Holy Spirit in my inner being. Keep me calm and reflective of Christ's love, no matter how annoyed I may be. In Jesus' name I Pray. Amen.

Day 23

Ephesians 6:10 *Finally, be strong in the Lord and in His mighty power.*

Human strength has its limitations. Even when we are determined to be strong, circumstances have a way of stealing our strength. There are many instances in pregnancy that call for strength. Daily routines can be strenuous as your due date approaches. Labor and delivery will take more strength than you can imagine and bringing a newborn home can also tap your energy. Thankfully, in this time of need, God will provide you with His strength to use as your own. When your body and your emotions are exhausted, you can turn to Him and He will give you the power you need to endure.

Lord, being an expectant mother is a joyous time in my life. I'm very excited about what the promise of this new life will bring. But even so, this expectancy is also a time of weakness. I have less and less control over my body and my life in general and I look to You now for Your strength. I can't do this alone. Please be my source of power and strength. Even though I am very excited about this pregnancy and this baby, my human joy is sometimes clouded with my human weakness. But I know Your strength Lord is strong and mighty. Please bestow me with Your glory. In Jesus' name I pray. Amen.

Day 24

Philippians 4:13 *I can do everything through Him who gives me strength.*

As your due date approaches you may start feeling apprehensive about your ability to actually give birth. In my own experience I questioned my strength and stamina and my body's capability to undergo such a strenuous event. I was also fearful about my ability to take care of my baby once I had to bring him home. Would I be a good mother? Would I be able to feed and comfort him? As all of these new concerns grew in my mind, I kept turning to this verse to calm me. I began to realize that I didn't need to be the strongest super mom in the world; I just had to look to God to strengthen me. And through His grace, that strength is renewed daily, and believe me I still need it.

Lord, I pray to You seeking Your strength. I am going to need it today, tomorrow and forever. There is so much I need to do physically to bring this baby into the world, and so much I want to accomplish as a mother. Lord, I know that I can only do those things through You. My body doesn't respond easily to pain and I will need Your strength to make that pain work for me in giving life to this baby. Strengthen my body, my mind and my spirit. In Jesus' name I pray. Amen.

Day 25

Philippians 4:19 *My God will meet all your needs according to His glorious riches in Christ Jesus.*

The difference between needs and wants is sometimes blurred from the human perspective. What you think you need, whether it's a completed nursery or more money in your checking account, is easily eclipsed through God's perspective. "Only one thing is needed," Jesus tells Martha in what I believe is one of the greatest lessons of the Bible for wives and mothers. In the end of Luke 10, Jesus and His disciples are visiting with two sisters Martha and Mary. While Martha is busy worrying about all of the preparations, Mary is sitting at the feet of Jesus, soaking in His every word. Martha becomes frustrated and complains to Jesus, "Tell her to help me." Jesus replies by telling her that Mary is the one whose priorities are straight. He teaches us that worrying about many things takes our focus away from the only thing that is important. And while Martha's dinner preparations were practical, we're talking about someone who fed 5,000 people with five loaves of bread and two fish. I think he could have taken care of Martha's dinner party.

Lord, so many times I find myself in Martha's shoes. Worrying about everything and everybody else and not putting my attention where it should be- on You and Your glorious riches. So many times I feel as though I "need" to get this done, or it "has" to be this way and I get lost in the details. Help me to focus on You daily and to see that You are the only thing I really need. Through Your Son Jesus Christ You have already provided me with all that I truly need. Remind me today and everyday that You will meet all of my needs according to Your glorious riches. In Jesus' name I pray. Amen.

Day 26

Colossians 1:11 *[We desire that you may be] strengthened with all power according to His glorious might so that you may have great endurance.*

Labor can last awhile. The average time span is about 15 hours. Some women labor for just a few hours others' have lasted more than a day. The general rule is that you will labor the longest with your first baby. A shorter labor will be more intense because no matter how long it takes, the process is still the same. Your cervix will begin to soften and thin out so it opens to ten centimeters. As the cervix dilates more, contractions will become more intense. Once the cervix is open, you will be allowed to begin pushing. Again the timing can vary from less than an hour to over two hours. Both of these phases of labor no matter how long they last, call for great endurance on your part. They are difficult and painful and best approached with the strength and power that only God can offer.

Lord, I know that I am about to face great physical trials. As my body prepares to give birth to this baby, I will undergo intense pain and hard, physical labor. There is no escaping it, I know. But I also know that You can strengthen me and help me face this challenge with Your power. Lord, I ask You to provide me with Your glorious might. Give me strength and power as I face these trials. Please give my body the physical endurance it needs to perform such a glorious undertaking. In Jesus' name I pray. Amen.

Day 27

2 Thessalonians 2:16-17 *May our Lord Jesus Himself and God our Father, who loved us and by His grace gave us eternal encouragement and good hope, encourage your hearts and strengthen you in every good deed and word.*

I consider giving birth a heroic deed and mothers the ultimate heroes. To go through such extreme physical changes and intense pain to give life to another person is a great sacrifice that hardly ends in the delivery room. It reminds me of someone else who underwent intense physical pain to give life to others. When Jesus gave his life on the cross, He gave us the gift of eternal life. Without His sacrifice we would never be worthy enough to enter heaven. Our Father in heaven is perfect and we will never be able to achieve that same perfection on our own. Thankfully for us, God knows that and has provided us with hope. Through Jesus' act of taking all the sins of humanity to the cross, we can be forgiven and can look forward to eternal life with Him.

Lord, You are the ultimate source of eternal encouragement and good hope. I rest all of my hope for my future and my baby's future in You. Please encourage me and strengthen me as my delivery day approaches. Give me endurance to bear the pain of labor and the strength to push this baby out into the world. Help me to find my strength in You in the first days of motherhood and throughout my child's life. I praise and thank You for the cross and for the eternal hope that it promises for each of us. In Jesus' name I pray. Amen.

Day 28

2 Thessalonians 3:3 *But the Lord is faithful and He will strengthen and protect you.*

Protection is very important in pregnancy. The safety of the baby before, during and after delivery is often the subject of expectant mother's prayers. But it is also important to pray for your own protection. You can pray for your health as you approach your due date, asking for protection from pregnancy related illnesses such as diabetes and preeclampsia. Asking God to protect your body during labor and delivery is also important. Delivery, whether vaginal or cesarean is a serious medical procedure and asking God for protection during the process is vital. You may also seek His protection from the enemy's attack, which may be emotional, filling your mind with fear and anxiety about the delivery process and your experiences in new-motherhood.

Lord, I need your protection everyday. But I feel my weakness even more so during this pregnancy. There is so little that I can control. I look to You today, putting this baby and this pregnancy in Your hands. I know that You are faithful. I ask You to strengthen and protect my mind, my body and my spirit. Bless the doctors and nurses on whose care I rely. Show them how to help me. Give them knowledge and wisdom. Keep me safe from any complications. Bless my body as it gives birth to this precious baby and encourage my spirit as I begin to care for him (her). In Jesus' name I pray. Amen.

Day 29

1 Timothy 1:12a *I thank Jesus Christ our Lord who has given me strength.*

This may seem like a verse to think of when it's all over, when you're holding your infant in your arms, praising the Lord. And this will be true. You will want to thank Jesus Christ, your Lord for giving you strength. However, just as His strength comes on a daily, hourly, sometimes minute-by-minute basis, your thanks can too. Jesus strengthens us everyday, even though we may only look to Him in our weakest or happiest moments. Sometimes events may be so overwhelming you forget to think of Him at all. That's why it's important to make our thanksgiving a habit, something we do automatically. The strength that Jesus Christ offers, is as helpful for overwhelming events, such as giving birth, as it is for the everyday strength we need to endure twenty-four hours.

Lord, I thank You right now for the strength You've given me, enabling me to make it this far. I need Your strength today and everyday. And I anxiously await the day when I can look to You in thankfulness for a completed delivery, for a healthy baby and a strong body. Help me to see that all I have in my life is a reflection of Your love for me and a gift from You. Let me make thankfulness and gratitude innate parts of my attitude. If I'm ever expressing ingratitude, please convict me of it quickly so that I can confess it and be renewed in You. In Jesus' name I pray. Amen.

Day 30

2 Timothy 4:17 *...the Lord stood at my side and gave me strength.*

Labor coaches often tell their "clients" to bring a focal point picture to the delivery room. This can be a calming scenic painting or a photograph of someone special, whatever the subject, the purpose is the same. It's something to focus on during contractions to try and get your mind off the pain. It didn't work that well for me, but I'm sure it works for plenty of women, or else they wouldn't keep recommending it, right? Anyway, while I was meditating on this verse, a beautiful image came to mind- a woman about to give birth, with a loved one with her and an angel standing by her side. Sometimes we forget the spiritual presence that is all around us. Firstly, that of Jesus: "Where two or three are gathered in my name, I am there among them" (Matthew 18:20). Wherever we are, even in a hospital delivery room, when we come together in the name of Jesus, He is there. And secondly, that of angels: An angel from heaven appeared to Him [Jesus] and strengthened Him (Luke 22:43). You can take a scenic photo to the hospital with you if you want, but be sure to take with you the image of this verse, that of Jesus and His angels, standing beside you, giving you strength.

Lord, I pray that You would strengthen me and that You would send an angel to be with me during the delivery of my baby. Lord, I believe that the most important being in that delivery room is You. And just in case I forget to pray to You in those hours, I pray now Lord. Guide me to the hospital. Bless the room and all who enter it. Keep angels by my side and bring this baby into the world in perfect peace and health. In Jesus' name I pray. Amen.

Month 8:
The Promise of Delivery

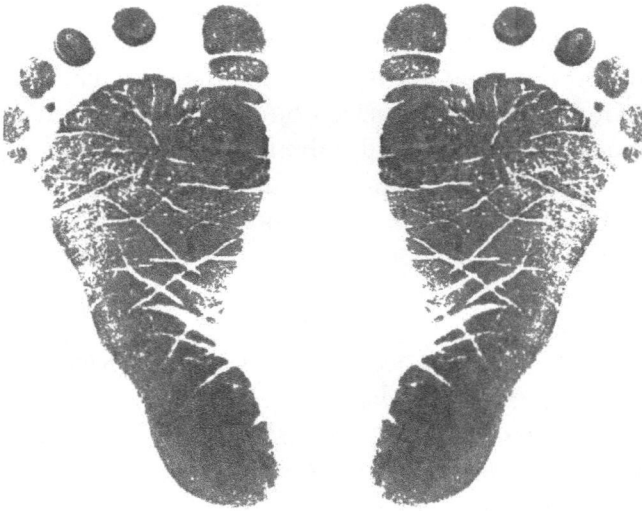

Day 1

Genesis 3:16a *To the woman he said, "I will greatly increase your pains in childbearing; with pain you will give birth to your children.*

I know this is a terrible way to start a chapter on delivery because for me, the most apprehension that I had was about the pain of labor. During my pregnancy, I was just looking for that one woman who could tell me, oh, it's not that bad, but that reassurance never came. It is that bad. This is the consequence that God set out for all women with the fall of Eve from the Garden of Eden. And you might think, well why should I be punished for her fruit-eating, but the fact is that we are all sinners. God has put this burden on all women as a reminder of the consequence of sin. And although you may not be thinking of this cause and effect relationship as you are struggling through labor, God will in fact use this process to bring you closer to Him. I can't think of another time when I have relied more on His power.

Lord, I know that because of the sins of Adam and Eve in the Garden of Eden, You have determined that all women should suffer while giving birth to their children. This suffering may even start before labor, as early as a couple weeks into the pregnancy. I pray that my degree of suffering would be as little as possible. Please give me the strength to struggle through this time and to bring a child into the world. I pray that my suffering would draw me closer to You and that I would rely on You for strength. In Jesus' name I pray. Amen.

Day 2

Deuteronomy 16:15b *For the Lord, your God will bless you in all your harvest and in all the work of your hands and your joy will be complete.*

One way that you can prepare for labor and delivery is to try and become mentally, as well as physically prepared. I use the word "try" especially if this is your first baby because being completely mentally prepared is an unattainable goal. You can never be fully prepared for everything that labor can bring your way, but you can try. Clinics and hospitals offer childbirth courses that familiarize both parents with the process of labor and delivery and may teach relaxation exercises and breathing instruction. Learning to reduce tension can decrease the pain of labor and make you feel better prepared for the process.

Lord, the thought of labor and delivery leaves me feeling apprehensive. I desire to be as prepared as possible for this event and I ask that You would provide a class or a learning session that would help to prepare me. I pray that my husband would be a supportive partner in this process and that he would be eager to take on any tasks that would help to bring me comfort. I ask that I would be able to train my mind to relax my body. I do not want to experience any unnecessary tension that could lead to an increase of labor pain. Lord, please provide me with the strength and skills that I need so that I can feel as confident and prepared as possible. In Jesus' name I pray. Amen.

Day 3

2 Samuel 22:2 *The Lord is my rock, my fortress and my deliverer.*

The Lord is our deliver. He delivers us from all of our troubles and He delivers women from their pregnancy with the birth of their babies. One way that this delivery can be prepared for is through a visit to the hospital where the birth is planned to take place. This will enable you to learn more about the procedures of the delivery room. You may be able to see a room, have the equipment and its uses explained, see the monitoring devises and become familiar with the various methods that are used to alleviate pain. This visit can make expecting parents much more comfortable with the upcoming event. It can even be used as a way to ask questions and raise any concerns you may have, as well as to explore all of the options that are available.

Lord, I want to praise You for the society that I live in that enables me to deliver my baby in the safety of a hospital under the care of educated doctors and I pray now for the women who are not as blessed as I am, asking that You would provide them with all they need to bring their babies into the world. I think about the birth of Your Son, who was brought into the world in the most humble of circumstances, even for His day and age and I thank You for all the options that I have available to me. I pray today for the hospital and its staff, asking that they would offer a safe place for my baby to be born. I ask that all of the equipment would work perfectly and that there would be no side effects from any pain alleviating methods that I might use. In Jesus' name I pray. Amen.

Day 4

Psalm 3:8 *From the Lord comes deliverance. May your blessing be on your people.*

When the Lord delivers us from our pregnancy, He is also relieving us from many of the discomforts of the last weeks of pregnancy. Most of the discomfort comes from the size of the abdomen, whose increasing weight can bring about back pain, pressure on the bladder that can lead to incontinence and difficulty in breathing. It may become increasingly harder to sleep at night because of the limited positions available (stomach sleeping is impossible and back sleeping is not healthy for a fetus that is near full term). The anxiety you may experience and the anticipation you feel towards the baby's arrival may also keep you from a much needed full night's sleep.

Lord, as You bring deliverance from this pregnancy, I pray for relief from many of its uncomfortable symptoms. Lord, please help me to alleviate my back pain and keep me from putting myself in any position that would bring an increased strain. I also ask for the ability to keep my breathing regulated and to be able to hold my bladder. I know it sounds silly but this is no easy task. Lord, I know there are many other symptoms that may cause me discomfort and I ask that through turning to You in prayer, I may find relief. In Jesus' name I pray. Amen.

Day 5

Psalm 22:9 *Yet you brought me out of the womb; you made me trust in you even at my mother's breast. From birth I was cast upon you; from my mother's womb you have been my guide.*

As of today, there are two ways to give birth: vaginally or by means of a cesarean section. Having experienced both, they are painful procedures and each has its advantages and disadvantages under each individual's circumstances. An emergency cesarean section can be given for any complications that may arise during delivery. It can also be scheduled beforehand if the doctor feels that some complications may arise, including the baby being in a breech position, where the legs or bottom are delivered first. Many women have strong opinions either for or against each of these methods, but the most important thing to keep in mind is finding a healthy balance between a birthing process that is as comfortable and natural as possible while minimizing the health risks to the baby and the mother.

Lord, You designed the human body to bring life into the world via the womb, but You have also given doctors the knowledge and ability to perform a surgery that would minimize any complications that a vaginal birth may impose on babies and mothers and I praise You for these technological developments. I pray that You would give the doctors the wisdom to make the best decision for both mine and the baby's health. If they decide that a cesarean section would be the safest procedure, I pray that the operation would be free from all complications. I also ask for a quick recovery. In Jesus' name I pray. Amen.

Day 6

Psalm 22:10 *From birth I was cast upon you; from my mother's womb you have been my God.*

Many Christians today can pinpoint a moment or a specific decision in their lives when they chose to accept Jesus as their savior and follow His teaching. For some it's like a flash of lightening, for others it can be a gradual process that takes place over a long period, or, if someone is raised in faith, he or she may not even be able to remember life without God. However, for each of us, our fellowship with God can begin at the moment of birth. David's experience with God began as soon as he was born and was continually strengthened from that point. The sooner we turn our lives toward God, the sooner we will be able to release our fears and cares to Him. However, the when is not as important as the what. God has control of our lives and waits patiently for us to make the decision to start a relationship with Him and then continues in His patience as we battle the sin in our lives each day.

Lord, I know that my baby will be cast upon You from the moment of his (her) birth, for You have been his (her) God even as he (she) grows in my womb. I pray that I would remember that You have full control over both his (her) life and delivery. I ask that Your providence would direct his (her) journey through the birth canal and into the world You have created. I also ask that he (she) would be quick to recognize Your role in his (her) life, that he (she) would acknowledge You as his (her) God and would accept Jesus as his (her) savior. I want him (her) to realize that following You is the only way to live a fulfilling life that brings glory to Your name. In Jesus' name I pray. Amen.

Day 7

Psalm 34:19 *A righteous man may have many troubles, but the Lord delivers him from them all.*

When I think about the righteous, no one comes to my mind quicker than a newborn. Paul writes to the Romans that there is "no one righteous, not even one" (3:10). However, I think that humans are as close to righteous as they can be when they are newborns. And yet, we hear of so many complications and birth defects that these little ones experience that we can become apprehensive about the power of God. Why would He allow such things to happen? Scripture tells us in Isaiah 55 that the ways of the Lord are not our ways. God's purpose is larger than our scope of comprehension and so as faithful servants we must trust that God will deliver them in His own way, from any troubles our babies might experience.

Lord, I do not always understand Your plan and purpose. However, I trust You and know that You will work all things together for good for those who love you (Romans 8:28). Please protect my baby from any birth defects. I pray that he (she) will be healthy and strong as he (she) comes into the world. If there are complications, I ask that You would grant all of us peace and strength as we seek Your deliverance from our troubles. In Jesus' name I pray. Amen.

Day 8

Psalm 37:4-5a *Delight yourself in the Lord and He will give you the desires of your heart. Commit your way to the Lord and trust in Him.*

Going into labor is a huge trust. You will soon realize, if you haven't already, that during your pregnancy you have little control over your body. The experience of labor belongs to your body. There is little you can do to speed it up or slow it down. And although there are many do-it-yourself tricks for bringing on labor, realistically, your influence is marginal. Even though we live in an age of scheduled c-sections and labor inducing drugs, modern medicine has not eliminated God's power or control over labor and delivery. The only true power available is delighting in the Lord, committing your ways, your labor and your delivery to Him and trusting Him to give you the desires of your heart- a healthy labor, delivery and baby.

Lord, this pregnancy has taken over my body. I can't sleep well and I'm uncomfortable. I lift my discomfort up to You and seek You as my relief. I also commit my labor and delivery to You, realizing that there is little in this process that I can control on my own. I put my trust in You today, knowing that Your power is mighty and asking You to bless my body and my baby through this process. Please grant me the desires of my heart- an uncomplicated delivery and a healthy baby. In Jesus' name I pray. Amen.

Day 9

Psalm 40:17 *Yet I am poor and needy; may the Lord think of me. You are my help and my deliverer; O my God do not delay.*

The length and time that delivery takes can vary from woman to woman and pregnancy to pregnancy. Time can span from hours to days based on numerous factors. And even though a shorter labor may be more intense, I believe that this psalmist is echoing the cry of a woman in labor, "Oh God do not delay." The pain of labor is inevitable but as God acts as your deliverer, you can seek speediness in His assistance. For no matter how long the process lasts, it is during this time that your body, wrought with pain, becomes poor and needy before the Lord. And with the promise of His delivery, you can look forward to a joyous ending.

Lord, I reach out to You as the Deliverer of all mankind and ask that You would also oversee the deliverance of this baby. I need Your strength to endure this process and I ask that you would grant it to me. Please think of me as I prepare for this delivery as well as when I call out to You during it. I seek Your help and Your deliverance and ask for a quick end to the pain of labor. In Jesus' name I pray. Amen.

Day 10

Psalm 71:6 *From birth I have relied on You; You brought me forth from my mother's womb.*

As women writhe in pain, labor becomes a perfect time to reach out to God for His strength and peace. God will strengthen and deliver you. However, He does not only hear your prayers as a mother. God also answers the unspoken and maybe even "unthought" prayers of your baby as he (she) endures labor and delivery as well. The traumatic experience of being thrust from the warm, coziness of the womb to the cold, harshness of the unknown is lessened by the presence of God. God's relationship with us does not begin when we are able to be cognoscente of Him, but rather at the moment that life first begins. He knits us together in the womb and certainly guides us into the world.

Lord, I know that the process of bringing this child from my womb will be painful, like nothing I've ever felt before. And although this pain is unavoidable, I rely on You to give me strength and peace and to bring the pain to an end with the birth of my child. I also ask that You would be with my baby as he (she) is brought forth from my womb. Please comfort my baby and keep him (her) safe as You bring him (her) into the world. And I pray that he (she) would rely on You not only in this moment, but throughout his (her) life on earth as well. In Jesus' name I pray. Amen.

Day 11

Psalm 107:6 *They cried out to the Lord in their trouble and He delivered them from their distress.*

Crying out is a normal part of labor for any woman. When we cry out to the Lord, He will deliver us from our distress. This is not to say that He will instantly remove all labor pain; the Lord's deliverance can take many forms. For me, the most effective prayer of labor was for God's deliverance from weakness and anxiety. Through His mighty power, He can give us strength to endure the pain and peace to rest in knowing that the pain will end eventually. And with the end of the pain comes the overwhelming joy of seeing your child brought to life in the light of the world.

Lord, I pray that today You would deliver me from the distresses of labor. Please make this a time when I not only cry out, but when I cry out to You, knowing that You are ever powerful, I desire to rest in Your peace and love. Just as I cannot bear any pain that my child might experience during his (her) life on earth for him (her), I am subject to the pain that accompanies labor and delivery. However, I look to You for Your strength, protection and peace, knowing that the fruits of my labor will supersede its struggles. In Jesus' name I pray. Amen.

Day 12

Psalm 119:170 *May my supplication come before You; deliver me according to Your promise.*

In the Bible, God makes numerous promises to deliver His people. He has delivered His children from slavery, enemies, illness and many other desperate situations. I can think of no situation more desperate than that of a woman in labor. As your body prepares to begin this process, you may seek deliverance from the pain just as much as the deliverance of the baby. By this time, your body may have ballooned in size and you may seek to see your feet just as much as you seek to see the face of your child. In all cases as you bring your supplication before God, you can be confident in His promise of delivery. No matter how long the labor, God's delivery is inevitable.

Lord, as I call out to You in prayer, I ask that You would hear my requests and grant me the desires of my heart. Please deliver me according to Your promise and Lord, please protect both me and my baby during this process. Keep us strong and safe. Help me to focus on You during labor and bring on a quick but safe delivery that glorifies You. In Jesus' name I pray. Amen.

Day 13

Proverbs 3:6 *In all your ways acknowledge Him and He will make straight your path.*

Preparation can be an important part of making the delivery process more tolerable. You can spend your last few pregnant days preparing for labor. This preparation can entail practicing breathing methods, elevating and soaking feet, ankles and lower legs, as well as cleaning and organizing the house to prepare for the baby's arrival. This last burst of energy is very useful because it may be one of the last times for a while that you have the time or the desire to house clean. Also known as the "nesting instinct," this is usually the last attempt at preparing for the baby. Although not all women may experience this to the same degree, I believe that each expectant mother is granted an extra amount of time and energy that enables her to mentally and physically prepare for the event ahead. When you acknowledge God in your preparation it becomes more effective. Asking Him for direction and the additional energy needed to adequately prepare for your baby will result in fruitful preparation.

Lord, I have so much to do to get ready for this baby. As much as I desire and anticipate his (her) arrival, I know that the event will be life-changing. I'm not sure what to expect exactly, so I want to be prepared for everything. Lord, help me to prepare my body, my mind and my "nest" for my child. I seek Your guidance in this readiness knowing that You promise to make my paths of preparation straight. In Jesus' name I pray. Amen.

Day 14

Proverbs 16:9 *In his heart a man plans his course, but the Lord determines his steps.*

Control- what a powerful feeling! As a huge fan of control, I often believe that the best way to achieve it is through thorough planning including list checking and goal setting. Plans are great tools, especially for maintaining focus. However, the great lesson of great plans is that their execution lies in the will of God. You may plan on having a natural birth or have certain expectations about labor and delivery only to find that little about the process is in your control. One suggestion that is made to expectant parents is to create a birth plan. This plan serves as a guideline for the doctors, outlining the procedures the parents want or do not want taken, as well as their general expectations about the delivery process. This can be a therapeutic exercise for the parents because it gives them a sense of control. What is more important to remember though is that all control lies with the Father, for it is He who determines our steps.

Lord, I know that You are the only one who has control over the birth of my child. And yet I know that You have given me the desire and responsibility to make plans for my life. I lay those plans, including our birthing plan before You. I ask that they would coincide with Your will and that the desires of my heart would beat in time with Yours. You have given me a heart that desires to make plans and I pray that You would determine my steps so that I may walk according to Your will. In Jesus' name I pray. Amen.

Day 15

Ecclesiastes 3:2 *There is a time for everything and a season for every activity under heaven.*

Timing is a very important aspect of pregnancy. As time passes, each week and each month brings differing stages of development. Everyone questions, "How much longer?" or "When are you due?" However, babies are rarely born on the date predicted. Doctors can schedule C-sections and use drugs to induce labor. An "overdue" mother can even try her own hand at speeding up the process. I've heard of 40 week-plus moms drinking castor oil, eating spicy foods or taking long walks in an attempt to jumpstart labor. Most of this desire to hurry labor stems from a hope of relieving your discomfort mixed with the anticipation of meeting your baby. Not every woman feels this impatience. When I was pregnant with my first child, I was quite happy keeping him inside in an attempt to avoid the fearful unknown of labor pains and with my second child I was quite happy keeping her inside in an attempt to avoid all the known work a newborn was! However, whether you want to give birth sooner or later is no matter to the baby or to God. For God has determined a birth date for your baby and when that day comes, there's nothing you can do to stop it or slow it down and little you can do to initiate it.

Lord, I have heard the phrase "God's timing" many times in my Christian walk. I know that You are in control of this birth and that You have already assigned it it's own time. My prayer is not that I would have the power to speed up or slow down this process, but rather, that I would accept Your will and the timing of the event. Whether I'm feeling discomfort, anticipation, anxiety or fear, please be my Comforter. You have chosen my baby's birthday even before he (she) was conceived and I ask that I would be able to rest in Your sovereignty. In Jesus' name I pray. Amen.

Day 16

Isaiah 9:6 *For to us a child is born.*

A child being born is the result of a woman's body going through a process called labor. Labor can vary in time and severity, but most women will say that it took too long and hurt too much. For women who have never experienced it before, it may seem too difficult to determine whether or not it has begun. There are some distinct signs of labor that will indicate the not so distant birth of a child. One of the earliest signs of labor is called "lightening." Here, the baby drops down low in the pelvic area, hopefully head first. This position has its good and bad points. Because the baby has moved down, there is more room for the mother to breathe. The shortness of breath that was experienced before will dissipate and deep breaths will once again be possible. However, the downshift also has a downside. An added pressure may be felt on the pelvis and walking may become more difficult (as if that's even possible)!

Lord, I know that in order for a child to be born to me I must endure the discomfort and pain of labor. Once my baby drops, I may feel more discomfort and even anxiety knowing that delivery could be weeks, days or just hours away. Lord, I just ask that You would bless this labor and delivery so I can rejoice in the birth of my child. In Jesus' name I pray. Amen.

Day 17

Isaiah 43:13 *"Yes, and from the ancient days I am He. No one can deliver out of my hand. When I act, who can reverse it?"*

This verse is encouraging to pregnant women in a number of ways. Initially it is a basis on which we can banish fears of delivery. As due dates approach so often do fears of complications. While it is true that there may be many problems that may arise during delivery, the truth is that there is little you can do to control the situation. You may find yourself relying on the knowledge and aid of professionals, yet more assuring is the peace you can experience when you rely on the power of God. No one can reverse His actions. This includes yourself and your worrying, which steals the peace that reliance on God can provide. Additionally, as you arrive at or even pass your due date, you can also rest in the message of this verse's promise. Once God wills it and acts- there is nothing and no one that can keep your baby from arriving, in His time.

Lord, please grant me the peace and patience that I am given as a gift from the Holy Spirit. I know that Your will for me is to abide in Your love and the peace and protection it provides. Your word says that no one can deliver out of Your hand. I pray that it is Your hand that guides my body and my baby through delivery. I also pray for the doctors and nurses who will help me bring this baby into the world. Please grant them wisdom and guide them in their work. I also seek Your patience. Please let me abide in this gift of the Holy Spirit. Help me remember that You will bring this baby into the world in Your exact timing and once that happens...who can reverse it? In Jesus' name I pray. Amen.

Day 18

Isaiah 46:3 *"Listen to me O house of Jacob, all you who remain in the house of Israel, you whom I have upheld since you were conceived and carried you since birth."*

Every move I made in my ninth month of pregnancy – especially any quick moves or motions that involved bending over- reminded me that I was carrying a child inside me. Each day that both she and I grew larger made the process of moving increasingly difficult. Moving as little as possible and resting frequently can provide some relief. I gained an additional sense of relief from knowing that I was not alone, for God's Word tells us that He upholds children from conception through birth and into life on earth. Using your body to carry a child can be physically and emotionally exhausting, but it is assuring to know that God is your partner in this feat. And God's carrying doesn't end at the moment of birth but continues eternally.

Lord, please help me to finish carrying this baby. As I grow larger this becomes a more difficult and foreboding task. Give my body strength and enable me to find a comfortable position. I know that You have upheld this child since conception. You have given him (her) life and caused him (her) to grow and develop. I pray that You would continue to uphold and carry my baby until the moment of birth and throughout his (her) entire life. In Jesus' name I pray. Amen.

Day 19

Isaiah 49:22b *...they will bring your sons in their arms...*

Although this verse is certainly not describing members of a hospital staff, the image of my child being brought to me is accompanied by the "arms" of a delivery room nurse. Not only will maternity ward nurses bring your baby to you in their arms, they will also be there during each step of labor. Doctors play a vital role in the delivery process but I found that nurses provide irreplaceable physical and emotional support. Maternity nurses quickly become labor coaches who encourage and oversee each stage of labor, trying to make the delivery as comfortable and safe as possible. Monitoring blood pressure, checking heart rates, helping with breathing and bringing ice chips are just a few roles that maternity nurses play in the labor and delivery process. However, I imagine their most fulfilling role to be introducing a mother to her newborn baby as they carry them in their arms.

Lord, I want to pray now for the nursing staff of the maternity ward. I know that nurses work long hours and night shifts and I ask that You would encourage them and increase their effectiveness. I pray that the nurses in my delivery will provide me with the emotional and physical support I will need during this time. Help me to appreciate their service and help them to see Your glory in the birth of every baby. As the nurses bring me my child in their arms, I pray that it will be a moment worthy of all You have created it to be. May each step of my delivery bring glory to You. In Jesus' name I pray. Amen.

Day 20

Isaiah 55:11 *"So is my word that goes out of my mouth: It will not return to me empty but will accomplish what I desire and achieve the purpose for which I sent it."*

Not every pregnancy ends in a delivery and not every delivery ends with a healthy baby. We live in a fallen world, far from the garden of paradise that God originally planned for us. I have no answers to the big question of "Why?" or "Why not?" but I do have the Word of God, which promises that God will accomplish His desire and achieve His purpose. God's greatest desire for His word and His people is to glorify Himself. When we pray The Lord's Prayer and ask, "Your will be done on earth," we are acknowledging that God's will is currently being done in Heaven, where God is constantly glorified. As you actively seek God's will on earth, you are asking for God to glorify Himself in your life and in your pregnancy. As you do this, you are not guaranteeing a perfect delivery and baby as the world defines perfect, but a delivery and baby that will perfectly glorify God in whatever way His desires and purposes decide.

Our Father, who art in Heaven hallowed be Thy name. Thy Kingdom come, Thy will be done on earth as it is in Heaven. Give us this day our daily bread and forgive us our trespasses as we forgive those who trespass against us. And lead us not into temptation, but deliver us from evil. Lord, I pray that through my delivery You will accomplish Your desires and purposes for me and my child. I ask that You would use us to glorify You. In Jesus' name I pray. Amen.

Day 21

Isaiah 66:7 *Before she goes into labor, she gives birth, before the pains come upon her, she delivers a son.*

As God speaks to Isaiah here and in the next few verses, He is using the birth process to describe His relationship with His people. This prophecy expresses the greatness and quickness with which salvation will come to God's people through Christ. A birth before labor and before any pain is a supernatural event- as is the salvation that Christ offers. God uses that birth process to create an extreme contrast. As humans we know that a birth free from labor and pain would only occur as a miracle. A similar miracle, not necessarily offered in the delivery room, is one of salvation. The labor and pain of receiving God's salvation has already been done for us on the cross. "It is finished" (John 19:30). There is nothing more we can add or subtract from it. Once we accept Jesus into our hearts, we no longer need to labor. "For by grace you have been saved through faith" (Ephesians 2:8).

Lord, I thank You for that salvation that has been given to me as a gift. I know that it was through Your great love for us that You gave Your only Son- that we might not perish but have eternal life. Jesus labored for us and endured the ultimate pain through His death so that we might be worthy to worship You in eternity. I thank You for that great miracle and ask that You would use me today to share this miracle with others. In Jesus' name I pray. Amen.

Day 22

Isaiah 66:8b *Yet no sooner is Zion in labor than she gives birth to her children.*

Some women have quick labors. We've all heard scandalous rumors of babies delivered at the prom- where the new mom hurries back out on the dance floor. That was the kind of labor I hoped for, I would joke with my friends. Whether or not those stories are true is not the issue here, nor is a quick labor in general- although it is something we can all pray for (not too quick though, you don't want to deliver en-route). In this verse, God is again using the labor process as a metaphor for His relationship to His people. If we look at this verse as a prophesy for the early church, we can see that the labor or work that the apostles did to establish the first church, quickly brought many "children" to God. With the presence and the power of the Holy Spirit, the early church was able to grow at an astounding rate. Without planes or cars or even trains- the Word of God traveled. Without the Internet or typewriters or books- the Word of God traveled. Without translators or dictionaries- the Word of God traveled. And even now that we have all these means of communication the most valuable tool is still the same-the power of the Holy Spirit and the prayers of believers continues to give birth to more "children" of the church.

Lord, I praise You for the power that the Holy Spirit has in the world and in my life. You are truly at work in the church body just as You are at work in my body. Lord I thank You for the child You have blessed me with and claim You as Lord over his (her) life. Please bless my labor and delivery. Make the process as quick and safe as possible. Let me feel as Zion did- that no sooner am I in labor than I give birth to my child. I pray that You would glorify Yourself in my labor and delivery, just as You did in the labor of the early church. In Jesus' name I pray. Amen.

Day 23

Isaiah 66:9 *"Do I bring forth the moment of birth and not give delivery, says the Lord, Do I close up the womb when I bring a delivery?" says your God.*

The promises that God made to His people Zion are ones that also ring true for pregnant women. Our Lord is the God of providence. In this verse, God is declaring His power to give birth to His people. He created us with the expectation of multiplying, and His church, as such, continues to grow. The Lord has not closed up the "womb" of His church. Everyday God's church grows as more children come to know and love Him. Just as God empowers His church to "give birth" to more members everyday, He also empowers women to conceive and deliver their own children. God has a plan and a purpose for each child even before conception- including yours. God doesn't just care for the growth of His church, but also about each member and each future member. And as He brings about your delivery, He is providing for His will to be done in the process.

Lord, I praise You for Your provision- You are the great provider: Jehovah. You have provided Your church with many members and You have provided me with the gift of a baby. You oversaw his (her) conception and I know that You will oversee his (her) delivery. You brought this baby into the womb and You will bring him (her) into the world. I believe that Your provision doesn't stop at conception- You will meet both of our needs right up until the time of delivery and beyond. Glorify Yourself in this birth. In Jesus' name I pray. Amen.

Day 24

Isaiah 66:11 *For you will nurse and be satisfied at her comforting breasts; you will drink deeply and delight in her overflowing abundance.*

This is a beautiful description of nursing a newborn baby but it is far from realistic. First of all there's the great debate of breast versus bottle, which I won't try to moderate here. Each has its own positives and negatives and should be explored on an individual basis by the parents. I found that breastfeeding worked best for me, one because it is healthy but also because it's quick and easy. But this was far from the case in the beginning. I was under the impression that because breastfeeding was a natural process, it would come naturally to me and my baby. However, I quickly found that at first it was hard and painful. I had to "teach" my son how to latch on correctly and "teach" myself how to be latched to. And because I couldn't see how many ounces he was eating, I became obsessed with watching the clock and I was shocked at how much it hurt. I had never read anything about that and thankfully a friend had told me to take Lanisol with me to the hospital, which did help with the irritation. But it took about a week before I wouldn't cringe at the initial latch-on. After many attempts, I soon found that both my baby and I were satisfied and comforted by the nursing experience.

Lord, there is nothing I want more than to satisfy and comfort my child. Please show me the feeding method that will best do this. Help me to feel comfortable and confident with my decision- for this is a strong desire of every new mom. Let our feeding times be more than just physical nourishment. Enable me to nourish the bond between parent and child as well. Help my baby to digest easily and let each feeding be a time of satisfaction and comfort. In Jesus' name I pray. Amen.

Day 25

Isaiah 66:12b *You will nurse and be carried on her arm and dandled on her knee.*

Here is another verse that uses the metaphor of a child to represent all of God's children. Is there a more satisfying image than a baby who has just been fed, resting on his (her) mother's arm or playing on her knee? The contentment of a newborn is God's metaphor for the satisfaction that He promises Israel. For an expectant mother, this verse serves a dual purpose. You can be simultaneously comforted in the satisfaction that God promises to provide for you as you grow as a member of His church and as you await the birth of your baby.

Lord, I pray today for satisfaction and peace for my newborn. I ask that my labor and delivery would result in a healthy baby and I ask that You would grant my child the peace and satisfaction that You used as a metaphor for Your church. Please give us peaceful feeding times and help him (her) to digest food easily. Please protect my baby from any reflux or digestion problems or dangerous food allergies. Show me how to provide the most comfort possible for my baby during feeding times. Open my child's eyes at an early age to the truth that the most perfect and satisfying comfort comes from You. In Jesus' name I pray. Amen.

Day 26

Ezekiel 12:23b *Say to them the days are near when every vision will be fulfilled.*

Although this prophesy is spoken to the people of Israel, I believe it resonates for every pregnant woman whose due date is approaching. So I say to you that the day is near when your vision of a newborn baby will be fulfilled. No matter how long your pregnancy may seem, it will only last nine months- ten tops. And as I mentioned before, I was reluctant to deliver- both times, for different reasons. Whatever your situation, sooner or later, an end will come. Every pregnancy will be fulfilled with a delivery.

Lord, You have promised to fulfill every vision- and that Your fulfillment will be near. I ask that You would give me the peace to rest in Your timing. I pray that as You fulfill my pregnancy with a delivery, You would bring glory to Your name. In Jesus' name I pray. Amen.

Day 27

Ezekiel 12:25a *But I the Lord will speak what I will and it shall be fulfilled without delay.*

A normal pregnancy can last anywhere from 38 to 42 weeks. If your baby isn't too large and the heartbeat is strong a doctor will usually let your pregnancy go to week 42 before he or she begins to induce labor. Inducing labor can begin with amniotomy, also known as "breaking your water" which is where the doctor inserts an instrument through the cervix in order to rupture the membrane. The induction of my first baby began with a vaginal insert called Cervidil®. This deposited dinoprostone, a medication used to thin and soften the membranes of the cervix. The Cervidil® was administered in the evening and then I was given a synthetic hormone called pitocin through an IV. The pitocin was used to stimulate labor. However, the contractions that it causes are often stronger and more painful than those of natural labor. It also makes labor constrictive because you are connected to an IV and a monitor for the baby's heart rate.

Lord, I know that You are in control of timing. You speak Your will and it is done without delay. If my baby's delivery is delayed, I pray that you would guide me and my doctor to make the right decision on whether or not to induce labor. I know that using medication involves risks, but delaying labor can also be risky. I want to do what is best for my baby. Please help me make the right decision. Guide us through every stage of delivery. In Jesus' name I pray. Amen.

Day 28

John 16:24 *Until now You have not asked for anything in my name. Ask and you will receive and your glory will be complete.*

Jesus tells His disciples to ask for anything in His name and it will be received. A quick reading of this verse made me feel simultaneously hopeful and frustrated. Hopeful, because I thought "Anything? Really? How about a new car?," and frustrated because I have asked for things, faithfully, and in Jesus' name, and have not received them. When we ask for things "in Jesus' name," is it just a phrase that we add to the end of our prayer request hoping to give it an extra boost and make it more appealing to God? I have to admit that this is sometimes true for me. But when we take a closer look at what Jesus is saying, we should redefine "asking in my name." When we truly ask in the name of Jesus, we should be aligning our requests and our own will with His. How could we ask for something in Jesus' name that was not in His will? When we attach His name to our prayers we should be making our prayers His will. And when we eagerly seek His will for our lives our glory will always be complete.

Lord Jesus, I thank You for giving me the honor to use Your name in my prayers. When I bring my request before You in Your glory, even the most important thing I can think of to ask becomes humbled. I come before You today and surrender my labor and delivery to You. I pray for Your timing, Your peace, Your presence and Your will. Guide my body Lord and protect my baby as You bring him (her) into the world. Let us rest in Your providence. Lord, I pray that You would glorify Yourself in this delivery. In Jesus' name I pray. Amen.

Day 29

Acts 20:24a *However, I consider my life worth nothing to me if only I may finish the race and complete the task given to me...*

In Paul's letters he often refers to life as a race- whether he's preparing his body or striving to reach the finish line. The main task given to each of us is to live our lives for Christ and establish an eternal home in Heaven- taking along as many people as we can with us. Although this is the main task in the "race" of life, it is accompanied by smaller tasks along the way, different "legs" of the race, if you will. As mothers we may see the main task given to us is to raise our children. Many times this task may seem like a race. We may grow weary or even fall down, but as daily inspiration, we can look to the finish line. The same is true of pregnancy. Each day may be more difficult as you stride toward delivery. And the last leg of this race is definitely the hardest, but as you keep the finish line in sight, holding your newborn in your arms, the race is worth running.

Lord, You have blessed me with a great task- bringing one of Your children into the world. I thank You for that opportunity and confess that I cannot do it without You. I ask for Your help in the race of life, in the race of labor and in the race of motherhood. Help me to endure. Give me strength and wisdom. Enable me to finish this task before me and give life to a healthy baby. In Jesus' name I pray. Amen.

Day 30

2 Timothy 4:7 *I have fought the good fight, I have finished the race. I have kept the faith.*

Paul makes numerous references in the New Testament to life as a race, with the ultimate prize being eternal life, but labor is also a "good fight" and when we finish the race we receive an amazing prize. The good fight of labor comes with the reward of a newborn baby. Keeping focused on this goal- what you've set out to achieve all along- will help you to finish this race. Seeing the infant that you've created and grown inside you come to life before your eyes is an overwhelming experience. When you have finished the race and are holding your baby in your arms, you can exhale with relief, knowing that keeping faith in God's power and providence over your delivery is what helps you maintain stamina in the race and what ultimately enables you to finish.

Lord, I will be so happy once this race is over and this fight is won. But now I come before You about to embark on this race of labor. Help me to maintain faith in You as I fight this good fight. Just as an athlete prepares his body for competition, my body has been preparing itself for delivery. As I begin this challenge, I ask that You would give my body the strength it needs to bring this baby into the world. Having the ability to give life is an amazing gift. I thank You for it and I ask that You would help me receive the prize for my laboring- a beautiful baby. In Jesus' name I pray. Amen.

Month 9:
The Promise of Joy

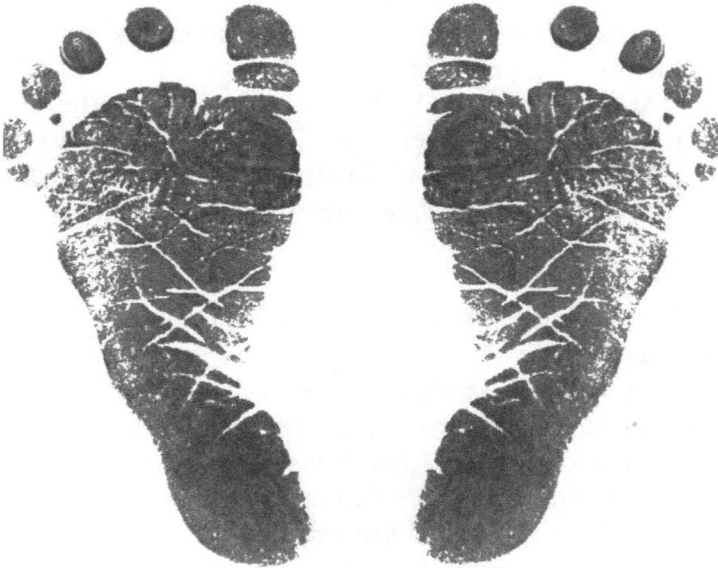

Day 1

Genesis 3:16 *"... with pain you will give birth to your children."*

There will be pain. From Eve, the first woman to give birth to the last, it will be a painful experience. It may begin with a highly discomforting pregnancy and end with labor pains or a painful c-section recovery. Hopefully you won't have both, but you will have pain. We can't escape the pain because it is part of the human experience. Adam and Eve represent the original vessels for bringing pain, sin and death to the human experience, but we are all sinners and so each of us will partake in the suffering of the human experience. The best way for us to deal with the inescapable is to look to God for deliverance and know that there is a greater joy that awaits us both in the delivery room and in eternity.

Lord, I know that a painful childbirth is the part of the consequence for the sin of humanity. And yet I call out to You today asking You to keep the pain from being unbearable. Please help me remember that there will be an end. No matter how long my labor or recovery is, I know that eventually I will hold a precious life in my arms, a life that was given to me by You. I ask You to be with me during the last stages of this pregnancy and to help me see Your glory in this experience. I ask that I would not labor in vain, but that this suffering would grow me and bring me closer to You. In Jesus' name I pray. Amen.

Day 2

Nehemiah 8:10b *Do not grieve for the joy of the Lord is Your strength.*

As we live our earthly lives, we know that we are not home. No matter how comfortable or uncomfortable our lives are, they are only temporary. These temporary lives can often be ridden with adversity. Through the course of our lives we will experience physical or emotional pain. And though this pain can feel overwhelming, it doesn't have to overwhelm us. God has provided us with an outlet for our pain: His comfort and joy. Any Christian who has experienced grief knows that God is the only true solace for such intense emotional pain. God also comforts us in times of great physical pain, such as labor pain. He doesn't remove the pain, just as He doesn't remove the loss or grief, but He gives us great comfort through His grace. The joy that comes with looking into your baby's eyes dims the pain of labor and will fill your heart with delight.

Lord, I praise You for all of the joy You have given me in my life. I have suffered and I have been in pain, but You have strengthened me with Your comfort and have enabled me to rejoice. Right now I am about to experience great physical pain. I need Your strength and the hope that comes with Your promise of joy. Help me to suffer through the trials of labor so that I may experience the great joy that awaits me. I am so excited to see my baby's face and hold my child. Thank You for the joy that lies ahead. In Jesus' name I pray. Amen.

Day 3

Nehemiah 12:43 *And on that day they offered great sacrifices, rejoicing because God had given them great joy. The women and children rejoiced.*

Once your child begins to talk, some of the first words that you might teach him (her) are "please" and "thank you." Every parent wants a child with good manners and requests fall on more receptive ears when they're preceded by "please." In my experience I find that I use the word "please" with God, much more than its partner "thank you." It's as if I find myself closer to God during times of adversity. If I'm anxious about something, or in pain, or upset I'm constantly turning to Him in prayer. It is the hardship of the situation that brings my thoughts to Him, but once the prayers are answered I know that I do not spend as much time thanking God as I did "pleasing" Him. It's important to remember that God is pleased with gratitude. He loves when we turn to Him with our requests for help, but He is just as delighted with our gratefulness. In Old Testament verses such as this one, the people offered sacrifices as thanks to God, rejoicing in all He had done for them. And although we don't practice the same way of giving thanks today, it is important to remember God's work in our joyful times and offer Him just as many "thank Yous" as "pleases."

Lord, I come before You today with an "attitude of gratitude." The ways You are working in my life are innumerable. You have answered so many of my prayers and I can feel Your presence guide me in my daily life. I thank You so much for this baby that is about to enter the world. This child is truly a blessing from You. I have turned to You many times during this pregnancy asking You for Your help, Your peace, Your love and Your strength. Today I ask only that I would remember You just as strongly during my most intense moments of joy. When the baby arrives and I am exhausted by the process and overwhelmed with all of the new experiences, I pray that when I look down at that little face, I would see a reflection of Your glory and turn to You in praise and thanksgiving, In Jesus' name I pray. Amen.

Day 4

Psalm 4:7 *You have filled my heart with greater joy than when grain and new wine abound.*

In King David's time, having abounding amounts of "grain and new wine" meant being financially secure, not having to worry about finding ways to provide for nourishment or pleasure. When we have these kinds of blessings in our own lives we can be joyous. Being financially secure can lift tremendous strain and burden from us. But as David tells us, and as many of us have experienced, that joy is dulled when we experience the joy of the Father. Having a lot of food or "things" will give us a sense of gratification, but there will always be something missing, we will always strive for more. Each of us is designed with an internal absence that we may or may not be aware of. And instinctively we try to fill that void. Some people may fill it with food or drugs or shopping or whatever. But those things, the things of this world will never be enough to quench the innate desire we have for the love for God. True joy comes from a single source.

Lord, I know that Your Word speaks to us many times about finances: how we can't serve two masters and how storing up grain and worldly things is pointless because this world is temporal. Lord, I do want to be financially secure. I don't want to have to worry about where my next meal is coming from, but at the same time, I know that true security can only come from You. Help me to see that even when I think I'm secure, all of this can be gone in a second. Lord, please help me gather eternal treasures. Show me where I turn to the world for fulfillment when I should be turning to You. Help me to live a full and enjoyable life here, but keep me aware of the eternal goal. Remind me that there's nothing in this life that's worth missing heaven for. I can't wait to spend eternity with You. In Jesus' name I pray. Amen.

Day 5

Psalm 16:9 *Therefore my heart is glad and my tongue rejoices; my body also will rest secure.*

After all the work of labor, what your body will desire most is to "rest secure." However, the restfulness of the post birth experience depends greatly on the delivery process. A c-section delivery will result in a few hours of rest in the recovery room. A vaginal birth may not be as restful, mostly because you're more aware of the process of the delivery of the placenta, which you also have to push out, or of stitches you may need as a result of an episiotomy. But after the delivery is over, your body will need plenty of rest. Of course you will want to spend time with your newborn, but you may also want to take advantage of the few hours you have with a staff of professionals offering their help.

Lord, I pray that my body will be able to rest secure after delivery. I know that this event is emotionally and physically draining, and just as the hard work is finished, I will want to spend time with my baby as he (she) experiences his (her) first moments in the world. Help me to balance my emotions and my physical needs. Enable me to experience plenty of guilt free rest, because I know that my recovery will greatly affect my ability to care for my baby. In Jesus' name I pray. Amen.

Day 6

Psalm 16:11 *You have made known to me the path of life; You will fill me with joy in Your presence, with eternal pleasures at Your right hand.*

Although this verse may not have been originally intended for expectant mothers, when you give birth to your baby, God truly is making the path of life known to you. You have known your baby's life from the very beginning and you know that its path is one of amazement. It will probably include discomfort, anxiety and pain, but with your baby's birth, you see where this nine month path leads you...to new life. The toils of this journey will end in the joy of a new creation, of a child and of a life filled with hope.

Lord, I thank You for making the path of life known to me. I have journeyed this far and I know that You will bring me to understand it entirely with the birth of my baby. You have planned a life of joy for me and I pray that this event will be joyous. Let all of my suffering and hard work leave me filled with joy. Help me to see that when this baby is born, it will be in Your presence. I also ask that I would walk with You on my life's path and that I would be able to teach my child to do the same. In Jesus' name I pray. Amen.

Day 7

Psalm 118:24 *This is the day the Lord has made; let us rejoice and be glad in it.*

This has really been my "theme verse" since my children were born. Whenever they're both crying or I'm trying to do ten things at once, or just feeling stressed out in general, I start to sing this verse to myself. I quickly discover that when I start to praise God during difficult times, the stress begins to dissipate. In the initial days of new motherhood, don't be surprised to discover that at 5:00 p.m. you're still in your pajamas. Some days you may feel like asking yourself if this cycle of bottles, diapers and burps will ever end. It is in these times that praising God enables us to see that each day is a treasure, that these moments will not last forever and that years from now we will look back on them fondly, wishing to spend one last night in the rocking chair, holding a newborn.

Lord, I thank You for today. You have blessed me with so much in this life. Even though some days are "bad days," each day is a gift from You. Please help me to relax when the stresses of new motherhood start to take over. In Philippians 4:11, Paul writes, "I have learned to be content whatever the circumstances." Lord, I want to share in Paul's attitude, please help me to be content in my circumstances as well. I know that in the next few weeks I may experience many emotions, from elated to overwhelmed and maybe even depressed, but I want to see Your glory in each day's circumstances. Help me to rejoice and be glad each day, knowing that my life and my child's are gifts from You. In Jesus' name I pray. Amen.

Day 8

Psalm 28:7 *The Lord is my strength and my shield; my heart trusts in Him and I am helped. My heart leaps for joy and I will give thanks to Him in song.*

Our true source of help during delivery and recovery comes from the Lord. We look to Him for the strength to endure pain and for protection from injury or infection. But on a physical level, much of our help comes from maternity ward nurses. I had a very supportive husband in the delivery room with me, but I was also glad to receive the help of experienced nurses. The delivery room is a highly stressed room for all involved. There are so many emotions at play that you may find yourself needing direct support from nurses. They can help to reassure you that everything is ok and encourage you to give "one big push." They will also help with feeding and baby care and can really boost your confidence levels with positive feedback and pertinent information. For parents, the birth of a baby is a pivotal milestone in their lives, but for the nurses, labor, delivery and recovery is also a job. It can be highly stressful, emotionally draining and generally exhausting. Therefore, you should also pray that the nurses that help you will truly be extensions of God's help.

Lord, I look first to You for strength and protection during my hospital stay, knowing that You will oversee which doctors and nurses I will come in contact with. I pray now that each one of them will help to make this experience a positive one. Lord, I pray that You would be with the medical staff. Give them wisdom and knowledge about everything involved in my situation. Help them foresee and avoid any problems that may occur. Let them be great encouragers and supporters. I pray that they will not be under stress and that they will give me and my child the best care available. In Jesus' name I pray. Amen.

Day 9

Psalm 30:11-12 *You turned my wailing into dancing; You removed my sackcloth and clothed me with joy, that my heart may sing to You and not be silent. O Lord my God I will give You thanks forever.*

I can't guarantee that giving birth will send you from wailing to dancing in any short amount of time, but you will certainly be relieved when your baby is born. Now, more than likely you will not be giving birth in sackcloth, however you might have to wear a hospital gown. Once you are in recovery, you can wear your own pajamas and comfy clothes. When you're packing your suitcase for the hospital, I recommend taking two sets of pajamas with button up fronts so that nursing will be easier. You should also pack a bathrobe and slippers because you might spend a lot of time walking in the halls. Be sure to include a few nursing bras if you plan to nurse and about 6 pairs of underpants. The hospital will kindly supply you with a crazy type of netting, but you might want your own comfy underwear and you might go through a few pairs during the first couple of days. You will also need a comfortable outfit to wear home, something with an elastic waist, and a cute outfit to bring the baby home in.

Lord, I would like first to praise You for the developments that have happened in the world of fashion, eliminating sackcloth from our wardrobes. In Matthew 6, Jesus says, "And why do you worry about clothes? See how the lilies of the field grow. They do not labor or spin. Yet I tell you that not even Solomon, in all his splendor was dressed like one of these. If that is how God clothes the grass of the field, which is here today and tomorrow is thrown into the fire, will He not much more clothe you..." (28-30). We are instructed not to worry about clothing but I would just like to pray today for preparation. Lord, I ask that as I am packing my bag I would remember everything that I will need. In Jesus' name I pray. Amen.

Day 10

Psalm 31:6b *I will be glad and rejoice in Your love, for You saw my affliction and knew the anguish of my soul.*

As you are gladly rejoicing in your newborn, you may begin to study your little miracle to find that he (she) is quite different than what you expected. Babies delivered vaginally may have misshapen heads or marks from forceps or other tools and procedures that were used during the birthing process. Their skin may appear puffy or swollen and may seem red or even yellow if they're jaundiced. It might take them a while to open their eyes and when they do, their eyes will probably be blue, even if no one in your family has blue eyes. True eye color can take up to six months to appear. You may also be surprised to discover that your baby has more or less hair than you expected. Babies don't usually keep the "hospital look" for long, but even so, I'm sure that your baby will be the cutest one you've ever seen.

Lord, I praise You for the joy and gladness I will feel when I see my baby for the first time. I'm so curious to find out what he (she) looks like. I pray that You would bless every part of his (her) body, just as You formed it in the womb. I ask that I would quickly establish a bond with this little one. I know that postpartum mothers don't always connect with their babies right away, but I pray now that no depression would hinder all the love I have for my baby. Please help us to fall in love with each other instantly. I praise and thank You for the miracle of this baby. In Jesus' name I pray. Amen.

Day 11

Psalm 51:8a *Let me hear joy and gladness.*

Although it's not usually a pleasant sound, the first cries of a newborn are one of the most joyous sounds I've heard. As an expectant mother, the health of your newborn will be your first priority and the first sign of a healthy baby is a strong cry. When a silent baby is born, fear comes too. As the baby emerges from the birth canal, a doctor or nurse will clean the baby's nose and mouth and suction away any mucus. After this, the cries will begin. Loud cries usually signify discomfort or pain, but a baby's first cries mainly indicate two things. First, the baby is responding to the trauma of leaving his (her) dark, warm, cozy home of nine months and entering a bright, cold world, with all sorts of new sights and sounds. And secondly, loud cries mean lots of oxygen going into the lungs, which is truly a beautiful sound.

Lord, I pray that my baby's first cries are loud ones. Please protect him (her) from being obstructed by the umbilical cord. Keep his (her) neck free from being entangled. Lord, create healthy lungs and airways in my baby and help my child breathe in oxygen and scream out in healthiness. I know that my baby's cries will soon become indicators that he (she) is unhappy or uncomfortable in some way and soon I may even be praying for him (her) to stop crying, but for now, for the first cries, please let me hear cries of joy and gladness, of health and strength. In Jesus' name I pray. Amen.

Day 12

Psalm 92:4 *For You make me glad by Your deeds, O Lord, I sing for joy at the works of Your hands.*

As you hold your new baby in your arms, and sing for joy at the work that the Lord's hands have created, you may notice a little hand gripping your finger. This isn't just a cute way for you and your baby to bond, it's one of a few involuntary reflexes that your newborn will have. This reflex, known as the grasping reflex causes your baby's hand to grip anything that you place inside it, the most adorable being your finger, of course. If you touch your baby's cheek, he (she) will turn his (her) head toward the touch due to the rooting reflex, where he (she) is instinctively "rooting" for food. Another reflex is called the stepping reflex, where babies look like they're ready to walk when their feet are placed on a hard surface. These are natural movements that God has created as part of your baby's instinct that will gradually fade away as he (she) gains more muscle control.

Lord, I praise You for creating this baby with these natural reflexes. You foreknew exactly what newborns would need for survival and created them with these instinctive movements. Your omniscience is reflected in all of Your creation, including in the new life of this tiny baby. Lord, I pray now for my baby's muscle growth. These movements are involuntary, but as my baby grows, his (her) muscles will need to be stronger and to respond to the brain's commands. I pray that his (her) muscle development would be perfect and that all of the muscles in his (her) body would work together just as You have created them to. In Jesus' name I pray. Amen.

Day 13

Psalm 111:2 *Great are the works of the Lord; they are pondered by all who delight in them.*

Sometimes I think it's the tininess that overwhelms us. Everything's just so cute. Anyone who's seen a size one diaper will ask themselves "Are they really that small?" And then there are the tiny clothes, not to mention the little socks and the shoes. However, no matter how adorable our baby's petite wardrobe is, it's the tininess of the baby that's amazing. When you unwrap your baby's swaddling blanket for a diaper change or just for a peek, you will be taken back by the smallness. Look at each toe with its perfectly formed toe nail and the little ears and the fingers as they curl around yours. They are all wonderfully created by a wonderful God.

Lord, Your works are great, but in my new-mother opinion, none as great as the creation of this little miracle. I do delight in Your glory, how You planned each part of this baby and brought it all to life in my body. From one tiny cell to a living, breathing human being, this entire experience is humbling and amazing. I am delighted so much by this tiny creature who slightly resembles me and I thank and praise You for giving me this precious gift. Help me to teach this baby how to love You and glorify You throughout life. In Jesus' name I pray. Amen.

Day 14

Psalm 126:5 *Those who sow in tears will reap with songs of joy.*

There is a chance that the difficulties of labor and pregnancy may bring you to tears, but I found myself crying only after the delivery. For me, I became overwhelmed when I first came home. I believe it was a combination of events. In the hospital, nurses are there to offer help and support, but once I was home I knew everything was up to my husband and me, no one was going to offer to take the baby into the nursery so we could get some sleep. Also, I was nervous that I wouldn't get everything right. Caring for a newborn is no easy task. When I brought my second baby home, I was hardly concerned about "getting everything right." However, the recovery from a c-section set off all kinds of emotions. First of all, I was taking pain medication, which left me feeling simultaneously elated and overwhelmed. And then I had a two year-old to take care of too. And he was also getting used to our new addition and missing a mommy who had been in the hospital for 5 days. My point here is this: coming home may take some getting used to. This is a huge adjustment for everyone, no matter if it's your first or last child. Don't be surprised if you burst out into tears at some point after this delivery. It doesn't mean that you aren't happy, it's just one way your hormones and emotions may chose to surface.

Lord, I know that this baby's birth is going to change many aspects of my life and my family's lives. I will be facing so many physical, emotional and hormonal changes that it's beyond a "roller coaster" effect. I prefer to refer to it as a tilt-a-whirl. Please help me to turn any tears into songs of joy. I know that postpartum life is not going to look like a Hallmark commercial, but I know that You meant for it to be a joyous time. Please help me to experience all the joy You have planned for me. Do not let any thoughts of insecurity, doubt, anger, isolation or sadness rob me from all the joy that Your will encompasses for me during this momentous time in my life. In Jesus' name I pray. Amen.

Day 15

Proverbs 10:1a *A wise son brings joy to his father.*

If a wise son brings joy to his father, I would say that a sleeping son brings joy to his mother. As joyous as those "awake" times may be, it's very important for new moms to get proper rest. Baby books will tell you that a typical newborn eats every 2-3 hours, so sleeping for longer periods than that are impossible, unless someone is helping you with the feedings. A good baby book should also tell you that there's no such thing as a typical newborn. Creating a workable sleep/eat pattern is an essential key to finding joy in new motherhood. Your baby's pattern should fit your lifestyle. Some people prefer the "baby demand" schedule where the parents respond to the baby. They feed him (her) whenever he (she) cries and let him (her) decide when and how long he (she) sleeps. I chose a modified "parent directed" schedule, where I woke my babies in the daytime to eat and play with the hope that they would sleep longer at night. This worked well for me but I know it's not for everyone. However you schedule your baby's nap and sleep time, make sure you take care of yourself too, by sleeping when the baby sleeps. Let housework wait. The best mom is a well-rested mom.

Lord, I pray right now for my baby's sleep habits. Dealing with sleep deprivation along with all of the other trials of new motherhood can be exhausting. Please help us to establish a healthy routine that fits our lifestyle. Let me get plenty of rest in those first few weeks. Please let my baby sleep peacefully too. Protect him (her) while he (she) sleeps. I pray that his bassinette or crib would be safe. Please protect my baby from SIDS (Sudden Infant Death Syndrome) or any other sleep hazards. In Jesus' name I pray. Amen.

Day 16

Proverbs 23:24-25 *The father of a righteous man has great joy; he who has a wise son delights in him. May your father and mother be glad. May she who gave you birth rejoice.*

A joyous relationship with your child may be based on his (her) wisdom in the future. But for a joyous experience as a breastfeeding mother, wisdom is also important. If you plan on breastfeeding, having an experienced "breastfeeder" as a resource will be very helpful. You will greatly appreciate having someone you can call up and ask some crazy and personal questions to. In the first few days of breastfeeding, the baby will be drinking colostrum, which is a thick, protein filled substance that is very nutritious for babies. After a few days, your breasts will start producing milk and you will soon find that new motherhood involves engorged and leaking breasts. Besides the Lansinol® ointment I mentioned before, it will also be helpful to have nursing pads and a breast pump. The pads will help with any leaking, especially since when nursing, milk comes out of both breasts at the same time- something I learned the hard way. And a pump will help you with any engorging and will enable you to store up a milk supply for future outings.

Lord, breastfeeding is a very natural act that will help me nourish my baby. I pray that it will come naturally to both of us. Please protect my nipples from becoming chapped, cracked or inverted and keep my milk ducts from clogging. Help me find at least one other supportive mother whom I can call with my breast feeding questions. Lord, show me the best way to nourish my baby and help me to be confident about our feeding times. In Jesus' name I pray. Amen.

Day 17

Isaiah 29:23 *When they see among them their children, the work of My holy name, they will acknowledge the holiness of the Holy One of Jacob and will stand in awe of the God of Israel.*

It has always been a mystery to me how any mother could be an atheist. For me, there has been no other event, no other process that has proved the glory of God more to me than giving birth. The transformation of one cell into many cells that form skin and bones and hair and eyes, not to mention the brain and the nervous system, the whole design process is awesome. Your body becomes a house for a living creature. Another human being, that slightly resembles you will grow and move inside of your body. A new mother's body will provide it with everything it needs to develop and grow for nine months and then it will naturally begin a labor process that will bring your baby into the world. There are so many earthly factors that could adversely affect this process that there is no other explanation for any successful birth except for the work of the holy name of God.

Lord, I come before you in awe and praise. You are holy. As I think of watching my baby sleep, I am in awe of You. You are the ultimate designer of the universe, from the massiveness of the universe to the delicateness of these ten tiny fingers and toes. Please help other parents feel the same awesomeness as they see among them their children. I praise You for the perfect work of Your hands and for all that You've done in my life and in the new life of this baby. I pray that we would use our lives to bring glory to Your name and to bring others to Your Son. In Jesus' name I pray. Amen.

Day 18

Isaiah 30:19 *O people of Zion, who live in Jerusalem, you will weep no more. How gracious He will be when you cry for help! As soon as He hears He will answer you.*

As soon as God hears you cry, He will answer you. This statement is sometimes hard to believe. I know that I have asked God for many things He has not given me. These may seem like unanswered prayers, but this is not so. Whenever you pray, whether it's a loud cry or a whisper, your prayer rises up into the spiritual realm and action begins. It's just that the results of the prayer in the physical world may not match the idea that you had of answered prayer. What you want at a certain time in your life is not always what is best for you overall. God may want to give you patience or humility as He answers your prayers or He may want to answer them in a better way, since He knows the future. Whatever response you get, knowing that God loves you and will answer your prayers in accordance with His perfect and loving will for your life, will certainly bring you joy.

Lord, I praise You for Your graciousness, for the help that You have given me in times of trouble. Even though I live in a broken world and have experienced hardships, You have always helped me. I ask You now to respond to me in the same way when I cry out for help during this time. As a new mother I will need help. You are the perfect parent. Please help me to be the kind of parent that You want me to be. Show me how to respond to my baby when he (she) cries out, just as You respond to me, Your loving daughter. Help me to accept Your will when it seems difficult or wrong and to know that Your love for me is never-ending and never compromised. Thank You for loving me. In Jesus' name I pray. Amen.

Day 19

Isaiah 35:10 ...*They will enter Zion singing; everlasting joy will crown their heads. Gladness and joy will overtake them and sorrow and sighing will flee away.*

You will certainly be in a more joyful state when your pregnancy is over and you are looking into your baby's eyes. However, there is only one place where you will experience everlasting joy- heaven. Life in this world is wrought with heartache. You may encounter worldly troubles of disappointment, sorrow, grief, and pain during your earthly life. Death is inevitable but your passage into heaven is a gift to you, provided for by Christ's death on the cross. Once you have accepted this payment, and Christ as your Lord and Savior, your admittance into heaven also becomes secured. Once there, God tells us through Isaiah that you will enter singing, an everlasting joy will crown your head. This joy will not be based on circumstances but will be something that overwhelms you. There will be no more sorrow, only joy and gladness.

Lord, I can't wait for the day when I will meet You in heaven. I can actually wait, but I anticipate my arrival in heaven with hopefulness. I thank You for providing me with a place where sorrow does not exist and I will be crowned with Your everlasting joy. During my life on earth, I have known joy and I have known sorrow and these experiences have left me with a desire to be home with You, overtaken with joy and gladness. I praise You for allowing Your Son to die for me so that my eternal life will be possible. I know that Jesus is "the way the truth and the life. No one comes to the Father except through Him" (John 14:6) I want so much to come to You Father and I thank You for giving me Jesus so that I can meet You. In Jesus' name I pray. Amen.

Day 20

Isaiah 42:14b *But like a woman in childbirth, I cry out, I gasp and pant.*

The delivery process can be filled with unpleasant sounds: cries, gasps and pants. These are the body's natural responses to the physical changes it's going through. These sounds will often accompany the "pushing" part of labor. The pushing begins once your cervix is dilated to ten centimeters. With each contraction, you will feel an overwhelming urge to push. If you are being administered pain medication, the dosage may be reduced at this time so you can feel the contractions and know when to push. This stage of delivery is very hard work especially since it comes after hours of labor contractions. Working with gravity may help. If you can you might want to squat or if you have to stay in bed, prop yourself up with pillows and grip your knees while keeping your chin down. Hold your breath while pushing, but take deep breaths of air in between each push. As the pushes start getting stronger, the top of your baby's head will start to appear and before you know it your practitioner will help guide the baby out.

Lord, I know that the pushing stage of delivery will be a difficult one. Please be my strength and my guide as I bring this baby into the world. Help me to manage my pain and to not feel embarrassed or restricted as my body responds with cries, gasps and pants. Give me stamina to push after the lengthy labor process. Help me position my body and time my pushes so that I will maximize my efforts and bring this baby into the world as quickly and safely as possible. In Jesus' name I pray. Amen.

Day 21

Jeremiah 31:13 *Then maidens will dance and be glad, young men and old as well. I will turn their mourning into gladness; I will give them comfort and joy instead of sorrow.*

God promises eternal gladness, comfort and joy with Him in heaven. But He will also give you glimpses of those gifts here on earth. When you mourn and are sorrowful, you can look to God, not to erase the events that led up to the desperation, but to provide an outlet for you. This life will be painful, but God wants to take that pain. He wants to turn your mourning into gladness and your sorrow into comfort and joy. While you are living on earth, God gives you a window into His glory. Just look at pregnancy. Your body goes through extreme, and if not painful, at least uncomfortable changes. Your body weighs at least 25 more pounds than it did nine months ago. You can't sleep. If you get sick, you can't take medicine. Your legs, ankles, and feet are swollen. Your back aches and your breasts are tender, sore and maybe even leaky. Then you begin labor: intense pain, rigorous pushing and maybe even some tearing. But when your baby is born you will be transformed into a state of gladness. You will feel comfort and joy. It will have all been worth it and you may even do it again!

Lord, I praise You for the eternal joy that awaits me in heaven. Thank You for being my comfort and my joy while I await eternity. I pray that gladness will overcome me as I look into my baby's eyes. And that I will see a glimpse of Your glory reflected in him (her). Please comfort me when my body is in its most uncomfortable states and strengthen me as I endure the trials of labor. Please let this pregnancy and delivery be a reflection of the joy that waits for me in eternity. In Jesus' name I pray. Amen.

Day 22

Malachi 4:6 *He [Elijah] will turn the hearts of the fathers to their children, and the hearts of the children to their fathers.*

It won't take much to turn your heart to your baby. An infant is so tiny and cute and helpless that caring for and comforting him (her) will be your pleasure. Who doesn't want to rock a baby to sleep? A parent's love for his (her) baby is a natural reaction. What needs to be prayed for then is the turning of your baby's heart toward his (her) Father in heaven. Jesus loved and welcomed children, telling His disciples, "Let the little children come to me…for the kingdom of God belongs to such as these" (Mark 10:14). I believe that human beings are closest to God as newborns and that the more time we spend in the world, the harder we have to battle to remain close to Him. He never leaves us, it's just that we can get easily distracted and develop skewed priorities. Children may not automatically grow into adults that love Jesus. It is the parents' responsibility to nurture that love. This can be done by simply praying together, talking about God, reading Bible stories and praying to God on behalf of your child.

Lord, I pray right now for my baby's relationship with You. I know that You love him (her) more than even I do and I ask that I will be able to help my child experience that love. I know that it is not Your will that even one of Your little ones should perish and so I ask now that my child would develop a love for You. As this little baby grows help him (her) to see the importance of having a relationship with You. Help my child to walk in Your ways and give him (her) a desire to know You better and love You more each day. In Jesus' name I pray. Amen.

Day 23

Luke 1:13-15 *But the angel said to him: "Do not be afraid Zechariah, your prayer has been heard. Your wife Elizabeth will bear you a son and you are to give him the name John. He will be a joy and a delight to you and many will rejoice in his birth, for he will be great in the sight of the Lord."*

Choosing names for my children was one of my favorite parts of pregnancy. My husband and I poured through baby name books, looked online and summoned the opinions of friends and family. The process is not an easy one. You have to agree with your spouse, consider all of the name teasing that may result from your choice and try to match the connotation of a name with the unknown appearance and personality of your baby. A Ruth will be quite different from a Chelsea. Zechariah and Elizabeth had no such struggles. When the angel of the Lord speaks to Zechariah about the birth of his son, he tells him to give him the name John. When the baby is presented, Elizabeth says that his name will be John. This surprised everyone because there was no one else in the family named John and tradition would have had the baby named Zechariah after his father. This passage indicates the importance of names. Here, God's choice of a name supersedes tradition and the expectations of others. An angel of God also tells Mary to name her baby Jesus. Recently, a friend of mine had a dream of God telling her to name her baby Gabriel. Names give us identity and many people have predetermined ideas about names, which they often like to share with expectant parents. And although God might not tell you what name to give your baby, you can certainly pray to Him before you make this decision.

Lord, You are a God of many names. Each one of Your names reveals to us something about Your character. When You told Abraham that You were I AM, You were indicating the scope of Your existence and Your power. As I try to choose a name for my baby, please help me to match his (her) personality with the perfect name. I know that much of my child's identity will be based on his (her) name. Show me what name to choose. In Jesus' name I pray. Amen.

Day 24

Luke 1:57-58 *When it was time for Elizabeth to have her baby, she gave birth to a son. Her neighbors and relatives heard that the Lord had showed her great mercy and they shared her joy.*

The angel of the Lord tells Zechariah that his son will be a joy and a delight to both him and many others. And when John is born, Elizabeth's relatives and neighbors share her joy. God knows how much joy parents find in their children, for He was well pleased with His son. But it is also important to point out that the joy of a newborn baby is not limited to his (her) parents. A new baby is celebrated by extended family. New grandparents, aunts, uncles, cousins and siblings celebrate in the birth of a baby. These are natural feelings of joy associated with the growing closeness of family. A new baby means one more cute and tiny member to love. The joy a baby brings doesn't end with family or with infancy. As your baby grows, he (she) will be a joy to friends, classmates, other adults. The extension of joy is limitless.

Lord, I praise You for the joy this child has brought into my life. That joy will be magnified when I see the way my parents and other relatives smile and coo at him (her). I know that his (her) birth will also bring them joy and I know that watching him (her) grow will continue to be a joyful experience. I pray that as my baby grows, he (she) will embody the spiritual gift of joy and that he (she) will brighten the lives of many people throughout his (her) life. I pray that others will see the joy of Christ in my child and will want to experience that same joy. In Jesus' name I pray. Amen.

Day 25

Luke 2:6 *While they were there, the time came for the baby to be born and she gave birth to her first born, a son. She wrapped Him in cloths and placed Him in a manger because there was no room for them in the inn.*

Let's talk about supplies. One of the stresses of new motherhood is making sure that you have all the "stuff" you need for a new baby. I became overwhelmed with the research. As my husband and I registered for our baby shower, he researched each brand and model of equipment making sure that we were choosing the right car seat, swing, crib, etc. It was a daunting task. But it was also something that we did together to prepare for the birth of a baby. If you plan on driving your baby home form the hospital, you will need a car seat. You will also need a safe place for your baby to sleep, either a crib or a bassinette. Diapers, wipes, formula and bottles (if you plan on bottle feeding) are also important. A few cozy sleepers, some burp pads and a couple of receiving blankets will come in handy. If all you have to make your baby comfortable in his (her) new home are the few things I just mentioned, he (she) will already have more provisions than our Lord and Savior Jesus Christ did when He was born. Swaddling clothes and a manger, it's quite a registry list! My point is, the things don't matter. Your love and care are all that your baby really needs.

Lord, I thank You for all that You have given me. I know that as I bring this baby into the world, he (she) will be met with more supplies than Your own Son was, no matter what. Even so, I want to have the best things for my baby. I want the safest car seat and the most comfortable crib mattress. Help me to choose baby supplies that will keep my baby safe and contented. Lord, You are the great Provider and I pray that You will continually help me meet my child's needs, both physical and spiritual. In Jesus' name I pray. Amen.

Day 26

Luke 2:9 *But Mary treasured up all these things and pondered them in her heart.*

As Mary cared for her new baby, she must have had many moments of joy and amazement. How excited she must have been to be part of the events that changed the history of mankind forever. As the events of her son's birth and newborn life unfolded, she treasured them, not knowing what the future held for such a miraculous child. I would like to encourage all new moms to treasure their time with their newborns in a similar way. One thing that helps me is a small journal that I keep on my nightstand. About once a month I jot down special moments and cute things that my kids are doing or saying. This helps me remember those special times, that go so quickly. Many times you don't have the same outlook on them when you're going through them as when you look back on them. Journaling doesn't have to be long or involved; it can just be a few quick words. It doesn't take much time and it will really help you treasure how God is working in the lives of your children.

Lord, thank You for all of the special moments that I get to share with my children. Help me to treasure those moments in the midst of all the chaos. Some days may seem like they're only filled with struggles and tears. Highlighting the special times will help me to reflect on all You have done for me and my child. As I watch him (her) grow, I want to see Your glory. Help me to follow Mary's example and take the time to treasure the fleeting moments of new motherhood. Everyone tells me how fast they go but I know I won't realize it until I experience it myself. In Jesus' name I pray. Amen.

Day 27

John 16:21 *A woman giving birth to her child has pain because her time has come; but when her baby is born she forgets the anguish because of her joy that a child is born into the world.*

   This is the verse that I based this chapter on. It encourages expectant mothers to know that through the pain and suffering joy will come. All will be forgotten. The joy that a newborn baby brings erases the pain that the birthing process caused. It's the reason why there are families with more than one child. As comforting as this scripture is to a pregnant woman, anticipating the joy of her baby's arrival, it was originally meant as an illustration for the disciples' experience. Jesus was letting them know that the grief they would experience would only be brief and that the joy that would come upon His resurrection would erase all of their previous grief. The same is true for you.

   Lord, as I struggle with the discomfort of pregnancy and the anticipation of labor pain, it gives me great peace to know that Jesus knew that this anguish would be erased with the birth of my baby. I know that we suffer birthing pain as a result of Eve's sin but at times it seems like a strange punishment. Lord, maybe You chose this way of entering the world so we would know what it would be like to enter the next. This world is filled with suffering and anguish but I look forward to the joy in the next life that will erase the pain of my troubles here. In Jesus' name I pray. Amen.

Day 28

Romans 8:22 *We know that the whole creation has been groaning as in the pains of childbirth right up to the present time.*

As Paul writes to the Romans, he explains that the suffering we experience on earth is only in anticipation of the coming glory. "I consider that our present sufferings are not worth comparing with the glory that will be revealed in us" (Romans 8:18). Paul uses the example of childbirth to explain this anticipation, but it is also a very helpful verse for an expectant mother. Your "present sufferings" in pregnancy and in labor are not worth comparing to the joy of your baby's birth will bring. Just as Christians "groan" in expectation of future glory, expectant mothers also realize that the suffering of labor results in a glorious future.

Lord, as a Christian, I am groaning. I anticipate a time when sickness, pain, disappointment, sorrow, poverty and all trouble will cease to exist. The glory that will be given to me as a faithful believer in the age to come is not even worth comparing to these sufferings. I thank You for helping me make the connection between this world experience and my pregnancy. I know that You understand the pain and discomfort and that You have ensured me that the joy that is to come will be much greater than any of the trials of pregnancy combined. Lord, please help me to focus on the joy that is to come. In Jesus' name I pray. Amen.

Day 29

2 Corinthians 7:4 *I have great confidence in you, I take great pride in you. I am greatly encouraged; in all our troubles my joy knows no bounds.*

Paul's words of encouragement to the people of Corinth ring true on many levels. At first I thought about the beautiful statement they make from a parent to a child. It would go something like this. "Dear child, I have confidence in you and in our relationship and I am very proud of all that you are. I have been greatly encouraged in all of this pregnancy's troubles because I know that the joy of delivering you and meeting you knows no bounds." But I also believe that these verses are a powerful statement to any expectant mother. Paul might not have intended for these words to encourage pregnant women, but they are effective. Anyone who has confidence in you and takes pride in you will inspire you to seek boundless joy through the troubles of pregnancy, labor and delivery.

Lord, I pray that I would feel Your love today. Help me to live with the confidence and pride that Christ granted me through the cross. Please encourage me through any struggles I may encounter as I bring this baby into the world. I desire so much to experience the joy that he (she) will bring into my life. I know that new motherhood is very difficult and I ask that You would help me to enjoy it. I want to share Your joy with my baby as I care for him (her) and as I tackle all of the chores and demands that new mothers face. Help me to manage my life so I am not overwhelmed by this new position. In Jesus' name I pray. Amen.

Day 30

Galatians 4:19 *My dear children, for whom I am again in the pains of childbirth until Christ is formed in you...*

As Paul writes to the people of Galicia, he describes his waiting as being in the pains of childbirth. He is waiting for those people to fill their lives with Jesus. He knows that when they do, the joy that will ensue will be worth the wait. The waiting is so painful for him because he knows how much they are missing without Jesus and because he loves them, he wants the best for them. When they do finally accept Christ's love, Paul will experience a similar joy to that of a new mother. He knows that all his waiting and praying will be worth it because the joy of Christ will dull the pain of separation. As you watch your child grow you will naturally want the best for him (her). However, just as God has given you free will, your child also has the freedom to make his (her) own decisions. Parental control seems to weaken in the teen years. Children start making decisions for themselves and although you as a parent know the right choices to make and want your child to make them, he (she) might not always make the best decisions. Each one of us has to choose on our own to come to Jesus and to let His will be our guide. Just like Paul, you may find yourself again in the pains of childbirth, waiting for your child to come to Jesus and follow Him, but know that just as your joy overflowed at the moment of birth, so too will it when your child chooses to have Christ formed in him (her).

Lord, I pray right now for my baby's salvation. There is no greater joy for a mother than to know that her children will be in heaven with her. I pray that my child will choose You early in life and will look to You to guide him (her) through life's many decisions. I realize that following You is not the easiest path, but it is the only road to eternal life and I want that for my child more than anything else. In Jesus' name I pray. Amen.

www.ingramcontent.com/pod-product-compliance
Lightning Source LLC
Chambersburg PA
CBHW022116080426
42734CB00006B/155

* 9 7 8 0 6 1 5 2 4 9 7 5 9 *